Toward

the End

of the

Century

Toward

the End

of the

Century

Essays

into

Poetry

Wayne Dodd

University

of Iowa

Press

Iowa City

University of
Iowa Press,
Iowa City
52242
Copyright ©
1992 by the
University of
Iowa Press
All rights
reserved
Printed in the
United States
of America

No part of this
book may be
reproduced or
utilized in any form
or by any means,
electronic or
mechanical,
including
photocopying
and recording,
without permission
in writing from
the publisher.

Printed on
acid-free paper

Library of Congress Cataloging-in-
Publication Data
Dodd, Wayne, 1930–
    Toward the end of the century:
essays into poetry/Wayne Dodd.
        p. cm.
    ISBN 0-87745-378-0 (acid-free
paper), ISBN 0-87745-256-3 (pbk.)
    1. American poetry—20th
century—History and criticism—
Theory, etc. 2. English poetry—
20th century—History and
criticism—Theory, etc.
    3. Poetry. I. Title.
PS325.D64 1992
811'.509—dc20   92-15642
                            CIP

96 95 94 93 92 C 5 4 3 2 1
96 95 94 93 92 P 5 4 3 2 1

Heaven and earth are trapped in visible form:
all things emerge from the writing brush.

— Lu Chi (trans. Sam Hamill)

contents

acknowledgments

Many of the essays in this book have been previously published, sometimes in different form:

"And Now a Few Words," "Dreams, Myth, Poetry" (as "From the Notebooks: Dreams, Myth, and Poetry"), and "Some Notes toward Sincerity" first appeared in the *Denver Quarterly*.

"What We Write About When We Write About Poetry" first appeared in the *Antioch Review*.

"And the Look of the Bay Mare Shames Silliness Out of Me," "Incarnations" (as "Incarnations/A Journal"), "The Art of Poetry and the Temper of the Times," and "Notes on the Line" first appeared in the *Ohio Review*.

"Fellowship" first appeared in the *Georgia Review*.

"Back to the Snowy Fields" first appeared in *When Sleepers Awake*, ed. Joyce Pesseroff (Ann Arbor: University of Michigan Press, 1984).

For permission to use copyrighted poems reprinted herein, the following acknowledgments are gratefully made:

"Loss," from A. R. Ammons, *The Selected Poems, 1951–1977*. Copyright © 1977 by A. R. Ammons. Reprinted by permission of W. W. Norton & Company.

"Taking the Hands," "Afternoon Sleep," "Remembering in Oslo the Old Picture of the Magna Carta," "A Late Spring Day in My Life," and "Driving Toward the Lac Qui Parle River" reprinted by permission of Robert Bly.

"Echo," from *Memory Gardens* by Robert Creeley. Copyright © 1986 by Robert Creeley. Reprinted by permission of New Directions Publishing Corporation.

"Delight in Singing," from *Eskimo Poems from Canada and Greenland*, translated by Tom Lowenstein. Copyright © 1973 by Tom Lowenstein. Reprinted by permission of the University of Pittsburgh Press.

"Because You Are Flesh," from *The Greater Leisures* by Jane Miller. Copyright © 1983 by Jane Miller. Used by permission of Doubleday, a division of Bantam Doubleday Dell Publishing Group, Inc.

"Spring" and "Winter Trees," from *Twelve Moons*, published by Little, Brown, 1979. Copyright © 1979 by Mary Oliver. By permission of the Molly Malone Cook Literary Agency.

"If It All Went Up in Smoke," from George Oppen, *Primitive*. Copyright © 1979 by George Oppen. Reprinted by permission of Black Sparrow Press.

"Gesture," "Of Being Numerous," and "Rationality" from *Collected Poems of George Oppen*. Copyright © 1974 by George Oppen. Reprinted by permission of New Directions Publishing Corporation.

"Rainbow" © 1974, 1975, 1976 by Stanley Plumly. From *Out-of-the-Body Travel* by Stanley Plumly, published by The Ecco Press. Reprinted by permission.

"Snowing, Sometimes" © 1983 by Stanley Plumly. From *Summer Celestial* by Stanley Plumly, published by The Ecco Press. Reprinted by permission.

"The Mind Hesitant," from *Collected Poems of William Carlos Williams, 1939–1962, vol. II*. Copyright © 1944, 1948 by William Carlos Williams. Reprinted by permisson of New Directions Publishing Corporation.

"To Flood Stage Again" and "Beautiful Ohio," from *Above the River: The Complete Poems of James Wright*. Copyright © 1990 by Anne Wright. Reprinted by permission of Wesleyan University Press.

Toward

the End

of the

Century

Fellowship

Under a fold of skin my right eye slants up toward its outside corner, giving that side of my face a slightly surprised expression. Or maybe it could appear a look of skepticism, or doubt. Or perhaps it suggests—what is in fact true—that I have carried forward into this present moment some of the genetic coding Choctaw Indians passed on to me through my mother, a dark and fiery young woman in the photographs taken early in this century by some itinerant photographer, Oklahoma then only a few years into statehood.

And all around her in the pictures, poverty as absence.

Absent too, of course, are the Indians, all those scores of thousands of Indians who, a generation or so earlier, had been herded into these 69,000 square miles called Indian Territory: Choctaws, Chickasaws, Cherokees, Seminoles, Creeks, Kiowas, Osage, Anadarko, Comanche, Caddo, Seneca, Potawatomie.... The roll call is long, the echoes endless.

What surely is present, however (visible even in so small a space as a front yard—fenced, of course, the glimpsed vacancy beyond) . . . What is present—in its level openness, the flooding light in every corner—is The Great American Prairie: the vast, mysterious reach of it, whichever way you turn; the lidless presence of it inside the body; the numinous feel of it in the spirit. And if you look close into the pictures you may see, in the young woman's frank and open stare at the camera, that droop of skin at the corners of her eyelids which hints at a measureless line of descent stretching back and back: the long journey of these eyes eastward and south out of Asia—across distances we now only guess at; across land bridges long ago lost to the sea; down through ice fields and ice ages, through eons of darkness and doubt, despair and courage, luck and ingenuity, and onto, finally, the vast and lovely plains of North America.

The prairie.

It spreads out endlessly before them, their camps beside its streams, on its grasslands, in the shadows of its hills—as ephemeral and numberless as the snowflakes, our own dreams as haunted as the prairie itself.

✳

Some mornings the slant to my eye is more pronounced— more surprise? more doubt? And I am always startled when, unsuspecting, I look into a mirror and see myself thus defined, thus questioned.

✳

My mother never fully acknowledged, I suspect, even to herself, the true extent of her Indian heritage, the percentage of Choctaw coding that was in her genes.

Today America is having a love affair with the Indian, now that the Indians themselves are gone (no matter that there are still some desperate and determined attempts by the scant remnants of a few tribes to hold on to the remaining bits of lore and practice, their fragile sense of tribal identity). But the truth is the Indians were always the enemy in America. And one need not romanticize them in order to identify most of the reasons.

They were, of course, in the way. They were an impediment, a block. They were in the way not merely of national expansion and prosperity; more importantly, perhaps, they were in the way of *individual* expansion and prosperity. It seems almost too obvious when stated this simply, almost too simple. But there it is, the simple core of it revealed: In this new land of astonishing natural abundance, except for the presence of the Indian, land and wealth and hope and freedom unlimited lay waiting for the individual—if he or she had the courage and the pluck and the determination to go and get them. In addition, of course, the Indians represented a relationship to the natural world that was, whatever else it might represent to the predominantly European whites, a constant source of challenge to the entrepreneurial zeal to exploit, to develop, to change.

Sell a country! the Shawnee chief Tecumseh once exclaimed. *Why not as well sell the air, or the great sea, as sell the earth?*

✳

Today we are surprised, perhaps, to realize how long this attitude toward the Indian persisted; surprised to realize that it continued until very late in the last century: until, in other words, the Indians were finally made unable to exist either as a physical threat to these goals or as a moral criticism of them.

And most of the Indians by this time had been "removed" to the future Oklahoma, where they would never again be allowed to be Indians, pursuing whatever call to living on this planet their genetic and cultural heritage might make on them where they now slept.

And where they now slept they settled, in a short while, into a pattern of failure and despair, poverty and depression, which robbed them even of that which had been, for the whites, their one enduring identity, one they could always, in a sense, respect: that of enemy. So by the early years of this century, they had come to be no longer hated, but merely despised. The fact that the image of the drunk and shiftless Indian staggering down the street or passed out in the censuring presence of industry and sobriety has become pure cliché in no way diminishes its truth. Indeed, it merely points to the simple and profound accuracy of it.

*

The fold of skin over the upper eyelid, anthropologists know, is a characteristic feature of the Eskimos, indicating that they are closer in time to the Asian races they are descended from than are, for example, the other North American Indians.

A few years before she died at eighty-two, my mother had to have plastic surgery on the fold of skin over her eyelids, which, always a characteristic of her eyes, had finally begun to droop so low as to actually interfere with her vision.

*

Some years ago, out of some circumstance I no longer remember, I happened to say to my small son that he was part Choctaw Indian. He became very excited, the idea of having Indian "blood" now a thing to be desired, not feared or despised.

"How much?" he wanted to know. "How much Indian?"

"I'm not sure," I told him. "Maybe one-sixty-fourth. Maybe as much as one-thirty-second."

It didn't sound like much and he quickly lost interest.

For my own part, I wondered what they could mean, those fractional amounts. One-sixty-fourth Choctaw: how can we measure it? Probably we can't—not in any scientific way. Still, I remembered having learned sometime that the adult human heart weighs approximately two and a quarter pounds. And a quick computation told me that one-sixty-fourth of my body weight yields almost exactly that much. Can I believe myself if, as I then wrote, I say, "My heart soared like a hawk to think so"?

✳

We live in a time and a society where success in public as well as private life is measured by the extent to which one can get rewarded for unabashed lying, either about oneself or about someone else. Preferably both. In such a setting truth telling grows increasingly rare, increasingly difficult. Most difficult of all, perhaps: to tell the truth to oneself. Or even to be able to know what the truth is: how to find it, how to see it.

For this difficult task, I believe, poetry is crucial.

✳

Late afternoon, a street in New London, Connecticut. We were slim and youthful in our dress-blue uniforms, four underage sailors. We had stopped beside an alley to drink straight from the bottle the searing whiskey someone had purchased for us. And it seared our stomachs as well as our throats, the gray winter light a pearly blur and shimmer through our tearing eyes, the universe centered, for a light-headed moment, on that nameless street in that unfamiliar city. A short distance away, the Thames River flowed past with the memory of all times concentrated and dispersed through its waters. And at that precise moment a young boy stopped beside us, and there on the sidewalk peered closely up into my face and asked, in a voice of wonder,

"Are you Japanese?"

The memory of World War II, then only a few years past, still concentrated and dispersed through the flow each of us at that moment was. In the failing light I laughed the laugh of fear and anger and ridicule and denial.

"How could he think such a thing?" I asked the night, over

and over again, the darkness deepening around me, my own beliefs and hopes all pure American Dream.

✳

So many things to understand, so many things we know almost nothing about.

Take poetry for instance.

For years I thought the great difficulty was learning how to have the poem mean what I wanted it to. And indeed it was a difficulty. But it was *a* difficulty, not *the* difficulty. Much harder, and much more important, was to learn how to find out what the poem wanted to mean. How to find out what I *didn't* know. How to listen and to look for what I had not yet discovered. How to be attentive. How to be patient.

How to accept uncertainty.

✳

Connecticut again, this time Middletown, more than a decade after someone had peered up into my eyes in racial query, asking, "Who are you?" asking, "Where do you come from?" asking, perhaps, "Where do you think you're going?"

And who was that someone, asking? Was it me?

I don't think so.

✳

Photographs of me at this time show a young man looking out of a background of certainty and accomplishment, a background of diligent and enthusiastic pursuit of a program of graduate study that still had the ambition (the audacity?) to possess all knowledge, to know it entire. To know ourselves entire. The Ph.D. had of course been inevitable.

As was my new career as a young faculty member at a large university, the final tracking down of the remaining facts and insights, my goal and my responsibility. My life's work. It is possible that in those photographs one of the eyes slants upward (in uncertainty? in dismay?), but if so, the dark horn-rimmed glasses hide it from view, and the eyes that look out from them seem absurdly sure.

It was a heady time. I had won a year's fellowship to the Center for Advanced Studies at Wesleyan University and had come, with my wife and infant daughter, to claim my future. Our future. *The* future.

✳

The Center consisted of two buildings set at the lower edge of the small "little-Ivy" campus of Wesleyan University. One was a small brick building, built expressly for this purpose. It was carefully modern in design, low-slung and long, and utilizing some large expanses of glass to offset the low and closed-in effect of the flat roof over the brick walls. It housed the main offices of the Center and the Center's director, novelist Paul Horgan. And it provided studies for a few of the Fellows. I remember that novelist and critic Hiram Hayden was there, along with Moses Haddas and Edmund Wilson.

The other building, a short way up the hill, had been built in the middle of the nineteenth century as a private residence for a sea captain who had commanded one of the many sailing vessels that sailed up the Connecticut River after their sea voyages to take anchorage at Middletown. It was a tall, stately home, with broad, columned porches, large windows (some mullioned), and three-story, white-clapboard walls running up to the many-hipped slate roof, which was topped off by a widow's walk. It was clearly designed for the wife of a successful and wealthy captain. From its height and comfort she must have often looked—expectantly, hopefully—down the graceful Connecticut toward the sea, everything uncertain in this life, of course, except, perhaps, her station in it; and even that at any moment might change, might already have changed, the name of her perspective perch offering insight into the future. Into, perhaps, the present.

In this building, with its large, high-ceilinged rooms, the rest of the Fellows were sited. *Sometimes,* the small booklet of helpful information informed us, *one might wish to have two or three of one's fellows in for sherry and conversation.*

I could easily have had them all in at once. My study consisted of a very large room, baronial in dimensions, with a Persian rug on the floor, some overstuffed chairs, tables with lamps, and two very impressive Elizabethan side chairs, massive carved oak and brocade. And, of course, a fireplace, though I never did get to have a fire in it.

*

On Monday nights, the Fellows all came together for cocktails and conversation in what had been the great salon of the house, its elegant chandelier testifying to the lucrativeness of this early form of the oil business, oil from the right whale lighting up these and other great rooms throughout eastern North America. After cocktails, we all went in to dinner, where we sat at one long table stretching almost the length of the very long room, while liveried waiters carried our food and wine to us, and we talked brightly through the brightly lit evening, other fuels now driving the turbines that generate the electricity that seems, at times, almost to have banished from our lives the ancient, fearsome night.

After dinner, and after we had returned to the comfort of sofas and chairs and soft lamplight in the great room, one of the Fellows would present a "paper" on the work he was doing—what he was writing, or thinking about. Usually it was the draft of a chapter of a new book, almost all of these great figures then in their prime and striding still, with confidence and the vigor of their achievement, across the culture of America.

*

Just how much of my racial coding is Choctaw Indian? I will never know. My mother always told me that she thought she was one-sixteenth, which would make me one-thirty-second. My father, who has known my mother all her life—grew up with her, knew her family, and who, at six years her senior, perhaps remembers them better than she does—thinks it was more. (My mother, like my father, was orphaned young, their parents, like countless others, having been placed in harm's broad way by poverty and the harsh frontier.)

"I think all those children were eligible for Head Rights," he tells me, meaning my mother and her five siblings. "But they were too ashamed to apply." He is referring of course to the rights of individuals to receive grants of land and sometimes cash, which the U.S. government had granted to specific tribes and which enrolled members could share in. To be enrolled, one had to be at least one-quarter Indian.

Perhaps it was as my father suggests. Perhaps not. It could be that my mother really didn't know. Perhaps it was her mother (one-half Choctaw?) who felt the racial burden most, the need to deny. But if so, think of the power of the need for denial, the rejection. All those young children, orphaned and not even dirt poor, just poor: first only one parent, then none—working a subsistence farm, staying together, enduring; economic and cultural deprivation the bitter taste they went to bed with, the daily taste they woke up to. A grant of land, a bit of money—it would have seemed like winning a lottery. And available to them, if they were one-quarter Choctaw, merely for the signing up? merely declaring their Indian blood? Perhaps.

But of course what can the young, orphaned early, know of the family's past, of families past; know of the blood that is thicker than water, and darker, often, than the very dark?

> All of them in the ground now, all
> In the commodious, American earth.

✳

Once, many years ago, a poet friend asked to see the manuscript of a book of poems I had been writing. When he returned it, a week or two later, he said, "These poems all tell me exactly what you feel and think."

I was very pleased. I assumed he was paying me a compliment, never imagining that he was speaking of block after block of houses without windows, houses without doors: no way in, no way out.

"Ambiguity," as Charles Simic would later write, "is the world's condition."

✱

The week after we arrived in Middletown, the autumn color not yet showing in the leaves of the great beeches in the backyard of our house, I walked down the hill toward the town's main street and a haircut.

The barbershop was owned and operated by the two Coronella brothers, but on this morning only Sal was at his chair. And so it was Sal who said, after some quiet snipping, "You're from the Hill, aren't you?"

"The Hill?" I said.

"You know, the college," Sal said.

I said I was. Sal seemed surprised. I asked him why.

"People from the Hill don't come down here," he said. "You're the only person from the Hill I've ever had in my chair."

The Coronellas were "town" people. And the factory whistles which came to punctuate our days and nights in Middletown were intimately connected to their personal lives and the lives of their families, sounding, for them, the urgent calls to labor and to rest.

Sal smiled in appreciation when, as I was leaving, I said, "Coronella—wouldn't that mean something like 'little crown,' or maybe 'coronet'?"

"You probably won't come back here for your haircuts," he said, "now that you know what's what."

We both laughed, and farther down the hill the river maintained the constant flow of its own dividing presence.

As it turned out, I didn't.

＊

Days I worked, as best I could, at the research project that had won me this spot. And I made steady if unspectacular progress. I also wrote poems. Increasingly I wrote poems. Had to write poems. I was not fully aware of the reason at the time, but clearly the poems were necessary to me. They offered me some contact with language and myself that made available more truth than was otherwise available to me. To be sure, I glimpsed it only darkly, if at all. Somewhere within this activity of poetic search, I must have felt, somewhere—beyond the fixed categories of certainty and definition and valuation— must lie possibilities of recognition and discovery which can touch more deeply into the subjective life we lead, the subjective life I was leading. But it was a largely secret activity, in search of an essentially subversive inner life.

＊

It could be plausibly argued, perhaps, that one of the early joys of parenthood is getting to read children's books to one's children. Which is to say, getting to read children's books: getting to share, day after day, night after night, those stories whose visions bring us comfortingly back—morning following, inevitably, night, even as sleep always comes, at last, to bring us relief and rest: the great rhythm of reassurance.

Of course it is also possible that the comfort of this vision can mask, for extended periods of time, other feelings your life may be creating in you. Feelings of loneliness. Feelings of desperation. Feelings of despair. What if, for example, your small child each morning, that vision's comforts still wrapped about her like a shawl, "See you first thing in the morning" sounding in her ears like the pulse of life—what if, each morning, she should rush to your bed, climb onto your chest, and recite the great mysteries of dreaming which the night has visited on her? What if, that is, listening then you hear—in your chest? in your ears? in the dark silence of the bed itself—no sound of return, no rhythm of rescue, but only the high whine of constant acceleration away, as if the entire small atomic group of you were speeding toward a dark present you do not want to wake up in, the dream of happiness only a faint speck somewhere behind you?

✳

Once some years earlier, when I was still in graduate school and programs in creative writing were almost as rare as Indians and thus not even known of, much less talked about, I "finished" a poem I had worked on for some extended period of time. I was feeling pretty good about it, thinking it a nice piece of work—a judgment for which, I now realize, there was no basis in fact—and I suddenly surprised both my wife and myself by saying that one day I would like simply to write poetry. Would like to be a poet. Spend my time writing poetry.

Did we both think I was crazy?

✳

Here, now, in Connecticut, I still knew what was what, and kept my gaze fixed down the road toward it.

At home meanwhile my wife, equally trapped inside an impossible dream of happiness, fell prey to one mysterious and disabling ailment after another: secret messages from the interior, calls for help neither of us was prepared to hear.

✳

On the morning Robert Lowell was to leave Wesleyan and drive back to Boston (or perhaps New York), I came upon him parked behind the Captain's House, a road map unfolded on the hood of his car, both it and his fair hair being whipped by a sharp November wind that had come up in the night. It was Monday. Lowell had come down to Wesleyan, as a guest of both the university and the Center for Advanced Studies, to attend the world premier performance of his translation of *The Phaedra*. There had been a dinner party in his honor at the Center on the night of the performance, and then, over the weekend, some other festivities as part of the celebration. Now he was preparing to leave and he asked me to help him find his way on the map—me, a relative stranger to New England. He seemed confused and uncertain. This was the time of *For the Union Dead*, still quite new; and *Life Studies*, which had won the National Book Award, was only a few years back. Now in his eyes, looking haunted and helpless out from behind his own horn-rims, one could almost see, if one had eyes to see, the source of these lines from "Home after Three Months Away":

> I keep no rank nor station.
> Cured, I am frizzled, stale and small.

Or hear, perhaps, if one had ears to hear, the echo in one's own self of these lines from "Man and Wife":

> Now twelve years later, you turn your back.
> Sleepless you hold
> your pillow to your hollows like a child;
> your old-fashioned tirade—
> loving, rapid, merciless—
> breaks like the Atlantic Ocean on my head.

All I saw, I fear, was uncertainty: his. What I didn't see was a life in shambles: mine.

*

Jean Stafford, for a few short months my neighbor at the Center and a frequent companion of ours in the evening, had a studio apartment in the Center, from which one could look out, through a large bank of windows, onto the town below and on down toward the river. We would sit there sometimes of a late afternoon or evening, two or three of us, sipping some bourbon and talking of mutual friends in Colorado; or of her cat, Hamlet; or sometimes simply of losses.

There had been Lowell, of course. And during the Lowell years, there had been the terrible car accident which marred her young beauty, and which she has written of with such lacerating precision and detail.

On one occasion I happened to have with me a copy of *For the Union Dead*. She saw it sticking out of my coat pocket and asked me to read a poem from it. When I finished she said, "That's me, of course, the woman in that poem." Then she pointed at another and said, "And there, too"—in the poem the lovers arguing through the night their intense intellectual pleasure.

And she was still fairly new to her role as widow of Joe Liebling, whom she loved to tell stories of, showing and savoring his great wit and elegance of phrase, while high above us the widow's walk, in the last light of day, mocked the speed with which we now receive the messages of disaster: *John Kennedy, shot dead in Dallas*; or the way we still gaze endlessly outward, waiting for someone, or some word, to arrive and ease our uncertainty.

Who could have guessed the losses that would follow? Jean, perhaps, who had long ago learned to escape the deceptions and distractions by which we hide from ourselves and from each other. Not me.

∗

A small band of people, maybe as few as three, struggle westward across the plains through the snow and freezing cold of December—in flight, perhaps, or maybe in some desperate attempt at return . . .

Is this familiar, persistent image simply a timeless and inescapable part of the American experience? Or is it, rather, the image of one particular family's flight, its ending still hidden in the presunrise darkness to the west of them?

✴

For a few years before, and a few years after, Middletown, I lived in Boulder, Colorado, then a small, fairly slow city at the foot of the mountains. A brilliantly clear stream—also named Boulder—came down out of the canyon above the city and ran right through the center of town and on out to the vast plain that stretches away in three directions as far as the eye can see, even from the vantage of an overlook several hundred feet above the town. Of course that is also what the Arapaho Indians, whose ancestral lands these were, saw when they looked out. And no doubt they too knew, as we do, that "as far as the eye can see" is only the tiniest part of it.

I don't know whether it is known what the Arapahos called the creek.

✴

The great problem for our culture, I sometimes think, is how to remember a future, how to imagine the past.

✴

"It is . . . a vision," Jung says, "such as will come to one who undertakes, deliberately, with half-closed eyes and somewhat closed ears, to see and hear the form and voice of being. If our impressions are too distinct, we are held to the hour and minute of the present and have no way of knowing how our ancestral psyches listen to and understand the present—in other words how our unconscious is responding to it. Thus we remain ignorant of whether our ancestral components find an elementary gratification in our lives, or whether they are repelled. . . ."

✴

A few miles to the north of Boulder, in another canyon down which water flows from the mountains to the plains, the stream is called Lefthand Creek, named for an Arapaho chief. But he was, like the whites, a recent inhabitant of the planet. What the Indians themselves had called it, no one now seems to know—this water that flows endlessly out of the snowpack on the high peaks, water that irrigates to patches of deep green the parched high prairie, while elsewhere throughout this vast portion of the continent the rivers carry their steadily decreasing flow of water, timbered islands now standing up out of their ancient channels, where horses and their riders once had to swim for their lives to reach the other side. And the great Ogalala aquifer continues to shrink alarmingly beneath the deep wells whose water is whirled and whirled, day after day, into the dry air, as we attempt to make even the desert green.

Meanwhile, Chief Lefthand and the great Oglala chief Crazy Horse, like my own ancestors, white and brown together, lie in the ground the aquifer diminishes under.

✳

Here I once lived. Here Jean Stafford grew up.

✳

One morning in Boulder I walked into the bathroom of my comfortable home and told myself a secret, a long-kept and carefully guarded secret. There with the mile-high air bright all around me I looked into the mirror of what we then called "the present" and uttered one mysterious, exotic word. And the secret was out.

Only I didn't know what it was.

"*Wakarimasen*," I had said, standing there in the clear morning light. And then, wonderingly, I repeated it: *Wakarimasen*.

Was it a question? Was it an answer? I had absolutely no idea.
I might as well have been speaking Japanese.

❋

Many years after I had moved away from Colorado, having
lived by this time for several years in Ohio, I wrote in a notebook some lines about waters and the mountains they were
part of. For I was—am—haunted by those waters, those
mountains. Haunted by their profound purity, the elemental
beauty they offer themselves as. Nothing soft, nothing pretty,
nothing touched by charm or sentimentality: just the essential
beauty of rock, tree, light, water, sky. I am drawn to them—in
memory and in periodic physical return—as an embodiment
of some elemental aspect of myself—of ourselves. They make
me feel simultaneously simplified and enlarged. Even, tempo-
rarily, freed.

So I wrote the following lines:

> Some days, in those years, I escaped
> into the hills that surrounded us, drove
> until the dirt roads ended
> at a wall of trees, then walked the morning sun
> up over pine and fir and aspen, up
> until the light reddened
> in the strawberries along the bank
> of the St. Vrain River, cast shadows
> on the rocks in patterns
> large as the house I'd left behind.
>
> Alone, I would wade those swift waters
> upstream all day,
> the slippery rocks and pebbles under my boots,
> hoping to feel again the . . .

This seems to have been pretty much the first form of it. A
start, an uncertain beginning . . . The strike-outs and -overs,

the super- and subscripts, the interlinings that followed—all point to an extended and perhaps intense time of trying to hear and see what might be present in these lines: changes that were clearly part of an attempt to hear the music better, perhaps see it better . . .

Exactly where the poem went after that I no longer find a record of. But I remember at some point "finishing" out of it a poem that was essentially all daylight and color.

Originally, it appears, the poem had gone aground in the shallows after "hoping to feel again the . . . ," dangerous waters at any time, for already that phrase is pointing toward some safe resolution, pointing toward an easy answer to an irrelevant question: "What did I think I had been 'hoping to feel again' in that poem?" That particular "completed" version of the poem, as I recall, seemed to feel that the answer was something like *the pleasure of being alone in the mountains,* joined to, perhaps, *the beauty of the "landscape."* Alas.

But of course that poem was "finished" in the way poems are often finished: as an act of desperation to have it over with. The desire to get out of it without too much loss (or discovery) simply overpowers one, because of one's inability to maintain what Keats called "negative capability"; because, that is, of one's inability to remain—at least for a while longer—in the presence of "uncertainties, mysteries, doubts." And so one turns to familiar associations and destinations, to comfortable and reassuring paradigms of our lives, to reinforcements of our prejudices, about others and about ourselves. And so we tell ourselves only what we already know.

Real discovery is always much more difficult to achieve.

The truer direction of this poem, of course, lay elsewhere, as I finally, after much searching, discovered. And it was not at all what I had earlier imagined it might be.

Here is the poem that eventually emerged.

BEFORE DIVORCE

Sometimes, in those years, I escaped
into the hills that surrounded us, drove
until even the dirt roads ended, finally,
up against a wall

of trees, then walked the morning sun
up over pine and fir and aspen, up
until light reddened
in wild strawberries along the banks
of the St. Vrain River

and entered, suddenly, the deep clarity of water
like fish flashing to the bottom
among shadows of boulders large as a house
full of darkness.
Some things are dangerous

to do alone:
go swimming, run a chainsaw,
be married,
fish a fast mountain stream, miles
from any road.

       It often comes down to just
this: your only remaining
ginger quill, your last chance
to salvage something
of the day your life is

is tangled on a cable angling high up
to rocks above the river, a long
hand-over-hand walk
above the bright water.
I was lucky. Hours later,

long after the day's last light had withdrawn
from the earth, and trees, beneath the pinholes
of stars, had vanished
into the hillsides,
I walked the uncertain trail back

to where I started,
the night so still my own
breath sounded like the wakeful
breathing of unhappiness
in bed beside me.

*

The only Indian word I remember learning from my mother
was *pashofa*. I believe it designated some sort of festival, a time
of rejoicing and celebration, characterized by feasting and singing and dancing. I do not know whether she ever actually par-
ticipated in this sense of community, this personal experience
of the word's meaning. But I doubt it. Mostly, I would guess,
for her its meaning was loss.

*

And what can most of us in America today, great layers of
concrete and steel and asphalt and artificial light between us
and the physical life of the continent, nature now only an
abstract concept—what can we know of the once elemental
power of the words for water and sunlight and the parent soil
to call forth the mystery of the living earth, to utter the wonder of our existence on it?

*

And what about, for me, *wakarimasen*? Of course I had in fact
been speaking Japanese that morning in Boulder, and I knew
it. For I had been to Japan once, not long after the time I
was taken for Japanese on the street in New London, my
eye slanting up then in still undiscovered doubt. And I had

learned a small amount of Japanese while there. But that had been a long time ago, and now, this morning, the language was all gone—except for, apparently, *wakarimasen*.

But what it meant, I had no idea. Indeed, so far as I could tell, it meant nothing to me: just a mysterious moment of language voiced suddenly into the air. After which, as Heidegger might say, the silent, nonverbal element continues.

Again and again I said it to myself during a long and busy day of work routine: *wakarimasen, wakarimasen*.

And then—the day having moved on, finally, to its familiar sense of unfulfillment—once again, uncertainly, *wakarimasen*.

＊

These messages we surprise ourselves to recognition by, potions poured into the porches of our ears as we sleep, our waking lives a shambles of borrowed aspirations, empty dreams, pointless achievements.

＊

Imagine a woman who loses the ability to walk. Say she is young, seemingly healthy, but her legs simply cease to work. Doctor after doctor, hospital after hospital, but no cause can be found. In one photograph, her husband is carrying her upstairs in his arms. In another, he is carrying her back down. If we held our ears close to her legs, or to her heart, the legs hanging useless over his arm, could we not perhaps hear that faint cry we always whisper to ourselves, *wakarimasen, wakarimasen*—already having found out the urgent truth of its meaning: *I don't understand.*

Now poetry becomes possible.

What We Write About

When We Write About Poetry

Let us begin by recognizing that one comes to a poem—or ought to come—in openness and expectancy and acceptance. For a poem is an adventure, for both the poet and the reader: a venture into the as-yet-unseen, the as-yet-unexperienced. At the heart of it is the not-knowing. It is search. It is discovery. It is existence entered. "You are lost the instant you know what the result will be," says the painter Juan Gris, speaking of and to painters. But what he is speaking of is true of art in general, is as appropriate to poetry as to painting. What he is reminding us of is the need to remain open to discovery, to largeness; the need to give over our desire to define, to interpret, to reduce, to translate. We need to remind ourselves, in short, that in a poem we find the world happening not as concept but as percept. It is the world happening. The world becoming. The world allowed to *be*—itself. Another way of putting the same thing, this time from the perspective of thinking (the perspective of the mind in its engagement of the world), would be to say that the poem is an enactment of think-

ing itself: the mind in motion. Not merely a collection of
thoughts, but rather the act of thought itself, the mind in action. The poem is not trying to be about something, it is trying
to be something. It is trying to incorporate, to realize. Not ideas
about the thing, writes Wallace Stevens, but the thing itself. As
Denise Levertov has said, "The substance, the means, of an art,
is an incarnation—not reference but phenomenon."

This is of course what gives to poetry, to good poetry, a feeling of aliveness. Touch its body—the body of this particular
"thinking"—and you will feel it pulse with hidden life. Which
in a sense is much the same as saying that it will pulse with
mystery. For what is more mysterious than the fact of life? I
mean life actually encountered, its own self-sustaining presence. What greater difference than that between a living being
and the corpse of that being, the life gone out of it? One moment it is a living presence of mystery. The next, it is something
completely other, something best defined by absence, by what
is not there. I can never get over it. At every moment I am
astonished by it. Touched by it. Awed by it. Perhaps that fact,
as much as any, is why I am a poet, why I have to keep searching for verbal bodies the mystery can be present in, where that
hidden life of the planet we are part of can be seen again. Can
be heard again. Touched again. And perhaps that reason, as
much as any, is why we need poetry, have to have it, have to
keep coming back to it.

Listen: *Oh, on a beautiful morning I think that I shall live
forever!*
Listen: *What's hard to remember is how the wind moved and the
reeds clicked*
Behind Torcello,
little bundles of wind in the marsh grass
Chasing their own tails, and skidding across the water.
Listen: *It is difficult to get the news from poems.*
But men die miserable deaths every day
For want of what can be found there.

Listen: *These come to me days and nights and go from me again*
       But they are not the me myself.

Listen: *Twenty-eight young men bathe by the shore,*
       Twenty-eight young men and all so friendly;
       Twenty-eight years of womanly life and all so lonely.

Listen: *That bareheaded life, under the grass,*
       Worries one like a wasp.

Listen: *Sweet berries ripen in the wilderness;*
       And, in the isolation of the sky,
       At evening, casual flocks of pigeons make
       Ambiguous undulations as they sink,
       Downward to darkness, on extended wings.

What we are talking about is the world's physical presence. And about our inevitable entanglement in it—our minds, our bodies. About the inexplicable capacity of words to embody the mystery of it. To actually embody it. Not just stand for it, or point to it, or suggest it: but somehow to be it. It is this quality of language—of words—that poetry throughout history has sworn its allegiance to.

In this respect, poetry is not so much a defining as a revealing. It recognizes the inherent mingling of the spiritual and the physical, i.e., the metaphoric nature of the world (or, as the Romantics would have said, the metaphoric nature of Nature). That is to say, it recognizes (feels, intuits, perceives) that the world both is and means. And that language both is and means. And that for us—human beings—language is involved in both aspects of it: both the being and the meaning.

And this is what we must give ourselves to when we come to a poem.

Most of the things we do to and with the external world have ulterior motives, have uses they wish to serve. And to this extent they are unwilling, or unable, to allow the world simply to be. Likewise language—always a part of our involvement in that world—is a part of our daily commerce with the world of use and purpose, of management and manipulation, of reduction and partiality. Poetry is where language can be released again into the fullness of its nature. Into its participation in the mystery. Into, in short, its metaphoric life. Likewise, poetry is where the world is allowed to *be*—independent of any designs we may have on it, any merely self-serving ends—and where, therefore, it is allowed to have inherent meaning.

But poetry is always more than mere meaning, more than mere use. Meaning is merely a familiar morphological structure it shares with other experiences of language. And use— well, use is one of our species' favorite categories of identification and valuation. One of its most impressive, of course. And also one of its most destructive. Both the medevac helicopter and the inevitable series of oil spills. Poetry knows use in both its guises, embodies it in its contrariety.

Poetry, I suggest, has no designs on the world. Rather, it manifests the desire, the need, to be at one with the world (which is to say, atonement: at-one-ment). A longing to be whole. To be unified with. To be reunited with. To be alive again to the world's living. To be alive to language's mysterious participation in that living. To enter the depth of it, the quiver of it, the dark knowledge the body has of it—its respiratory involvement in the rhythms of it: the music of being.

What does this tell us about the close reading of poems, and about writing about poems? Well, it tells us something about what not to do, something about how not to approach a poem. But more importantly, it gives us some sense of where we might look as we try to talk to ourselves about the journey the poem is. An uncertain sense, to be sure (we are after all trying to talk about something that has mystery at the heart of it, and mystery is by definition not susceptible to explanation or solution)—but a sense nonetheless. We recognize that what we want most in a poem is the feeling that it has life in it, something that is not expressible by mere "writing."

Consider Mary Oliver's poem "Spring":

> In April the Morgan was bred. I was chased away.
> I heard the cries of the horses where I waited,
> And the laughter of the men.

> Later the farmer who owned the stallion
> Found me and said, "She's done.
> You tell your daddy he owes me fifty dollars."
>
> I rode her home at her leisure
> And let her, wherever she wanted,
> Tear with her huge teeth, roughly,
>
> Blades from the fields of spring.

Always the question for art is, it seems to me, how to make the moment existential, how to make it a living moment of the world. Here Mary Oliver listens, with her poem, to the great echo in the blood the seasons and the irresistible drive of sex make together. We enter it and we feel it, its deep pulse and motion. And our bodies ripple with their dark knowledge of it, the rhythms we share together on the earth, their great ease and fulfillment, the delicate violence the flesh is heir to.

> And let her, wherever she wanted,
> Tear with her huge teeth, roughly,
>
> Blades from the fields of spring.

What is central here is the certain knowledge the words have—that our bodies have—of cropping (Tear with her huge teeth, roughly) and chewing (Blades from the fields of spring)—the ruminative way the words, in their physical presence, feel that knowledge, those activities.

And of course there is the poem's eloquent, silent recognition (made not so much by the speaker as in and through her): namely, the kinship of flesh and flesh, the awesome mystery our shared physical life is.

And here is Oliver's poem "Winter Trees":

> First it was only the winter trees—
> their boughs eloquent at midnight
>
> with small but mortal explosions, and always a humming
> under the lashings of storm.

Nights I sat at the kitchen door
listening out into the darkness

until finally spring came, and everything
transcended. As one by one

the ponds opened, took the white ice
painfully into their dark bellies,

I began to listen to them shore-slapping and rock-leaping
into the growl of creeks,

and then of course the ocean, far off,
pouring everything, over and over,

from jar to enormous jar. You'd think
it would stop somewhere, but next it was rocks,

flicking their silver tongues all summer, panting
a little on their damp under-sides.

Now I listen as fall rides
in the wagons of the wind, lighting up the world

with red, yellow, and the long-leaved ash
as blue as fire, and I know

there's no end to it, the kingdoms
crying out—and no end

to the voices the heart can hear once
it's started. Already like small white birds

snow is falling from the ledges of the north, each flake
singing with its tiny mouth as it wings out

into the wind, whispering about love, about darkness
as it balances in the clear air, as it whirls down.

Of course this is a beautiful poem, perhaps a more compelling poem than "Spring" (I won't say a "better" poem). And we could begin talking about it from many different angles. But I think a particularly interesting way of "thinking about" this poem (having already given ourselves to its immediacy, its living presence) would be to talk about—to think about—its language. The way, for example, the poem comes to say/dares to say, "the voices the heart can hear," all of us knowing that the heart as a seat of the emotions is a much-mauled metaphor by now, one coarsened by the roar and grind of thousands of trucks along the endless highways of America, battered and smudged and lacerated by great strips and chunks of the immense tires our lives ride—and explode—on, always en route to Nashville. And we know, as Donald Barthelme has eloquently said, that one of poetry's central, one of its crucial, projects is "restoring freshness to a much-handled language." The problem for the poet is to find a language one can believe in, one in which there is an opportunity to hear something that is not merely comfortably familiar, not merely reinforcing of one's own prejudices or assumptions.

It is always so, has always been so, though perhaps it is even harder today—with the everpresent pressure from our devouring commercial culture, our technology of hype and manipulation.

How can one be sincere? How do we find a clean language, one free of political and social contamination?

It is first necessary, always, "to silence an existing rhetoric" (Barthelme)—necessary to clear the mouth and the throat and the ears. It is necessary to listen: to what makes available to us more than mere schemes and rationalizations, strategies and maneuvers. We must let the world in, in complexity and contrariety. And "The world enters the work as it enters our ordinary lives, not as world-view or system but in sharp particularity."

> First it was only the winter trees—
> their boughs eloquent at midnight
>
> with small but mortal explosions, and always a humming
> under the lashings of the storm.

As always, the world has entered the poem—has entered us—as that inseparable mixture of things and words. Has entered the poet's memory and mouth, has entered her body's unconscious harmony with the physical realm we all are part of, which we wake and sleep on, its autonomic oneness.

As one by one

the ponds opened, took the white ice
painfully into their dark bellies,

I began to listen to them shore-slapping and rock-leaping
into the growl of creeks,

and then of course the ocean, far off,
pouring everything, over and over,

from jar to enormous jar.

What these lines know is as much the body's knowledge as the mind's; more, even. And the words speak that knowledge, vibrate with its physicality. We're not talking here of some instance of cleverness on the part of the poet, not pointing to some poetic device involving sound manipulation, not merely noting the sound of water in "shore-slapping and rock-leaping." We're talking about how the life of the body (ours and the rest of the world's)—how the life of the body is somehow in them. In the words. How water, as both environment and constituent of the body itself, echoes in the lines. In us. How it is both foreground (in the growl of creeks) and the immortal element itself, water, stretching and pouring, "over and over, / from jar to enormous jar," our lives forever caught up in the vastness of it, the resistless run of it, around us and through us. And inherent in all this—*inherent* in all this—the great roll of the seasons, known to all our senses: the very fact of Time incarnated, in this and in us.

We read these lines, listen to their music of presence, and the world is alive in it—alive in us—our quiet fellow citizens the rocks "flicking their silver tongues all summer, panting / a little on their damp undersides." Already, we know, "like small white birds / / snow is falling," each flake, each word knowing their great fragility, the vulnerability of our brief launchings into flight, the desperate courage each winging out floats on, trusts to. Nothing is about anything: everything *is*. But it is, of course, in time: actually *in* time, its poignant tug and pull. So when suddenly we, as the poem, say there is "no end / / to the voices the heart can hear once / it's started," we are saying the literal truth this poem has found out: the *literal* heart, with its dark, venous connections to the voices life sounds through us, their brief moments in time: the voices—the body—"whispering about love, about darkness / as it balances in the clear air, as it whirls down."

The literal heart. Its physical truth. And so, therefore, instinct with metaphor.

✳

Where the life is—in the poem. The signs of its presence. That's what we're talking about. This, I am suggesting—this mysterious presence—is a touchstone of something. If it is there, however difficult it may be to devise an adequate language to describe it, then we believe in it; believe reality is in it; believe being is in it; believe it is an instance of—to borrow a phrase from Heidegger—world worlding. In other words, we believe it is art. If, however, we are unable, no matter how attentive we are, to find this presence of life in it—in that case we are likely to say that what we are faced with is a failed poem.

What we are talking about, therefore, is that which is most important for us to find in a poem, and, if we are going to talk about it, that which is most important for us to talk (or write) about. It is what we must never remove, or kill off, by translating the poem into some other mode of discourse. This presence seems to be at the heart of the matter and so must be preserved and respected at all costs when we speak of the poem.

What is of primary importance is that poems should not—

must not—be translated into some mere category; they must not be reduced to only an aspect of themselves—of ourselves. They must not be only what we already know (or "understand," or are able to explain). Poems are never merely. That is to say, they have being rather than meaning. They are their own uses. They are not resolved, they are entered. Poems are where, physically, our own bodies and the bodies of words join in reality's pulse and movement. They are where, physically and spiritually, our existence is entered, in its mysterious fullness. Poetry is not a saying: it is a becoming. It is never an errand, at the service of some other need or value: it is a journey into. It is existence entered.

Consider the small poem "Loss," by A. R. Ammons:

> When the sun
> falls behind the sumac
> thicket the
> wild
> yellow daisies
> in diffuse evening shade
> lose their
> rigorous attention
> and
> half-wild with loss
> turn
> any way the wind does
> and lift their
> petals up
> to float
> off their stems
> and go

What a deceptively simple little poem. Which is to say, it *looks* simple, if you are used to seeing poems with longer lines, or if you expect serious poems to have more lines, or if your habit of mind is always to read a poem for a detachable "content"—meaning, I suppose, some paraphrasable thought, that which, in other words, can be abstracted from the dense tangle of singularity an actual poem is, an actual life is. But remember: as Robert Creeley says, "A poetry denies its end in any descriptive act, I mean an act which leaves the attention outside the poem." How inversely apposite Ammons's poem is. This poem is so fully a reproduction of "the act of the world on consciousness" that the moment which it appears as is itself the very presence of ephemerality. Again and again we read it, follow its pure and subtle rhythms to the petals' inevitable departure: and still we have to return to it, have to go through it again, to experience the enactment of loss—our minds, our eyes, our tongues tangled fast in this intense presence of the material world, the quick moment of truth—that wonderful line "half-wild with loss" holding us, defining us. God, I love that line: half-wild with loss. It privileges the rest of the poem, and is privileged by it. The exquisite brevity of this moment-in-the-sun *moves* in this poem, and it moves in us—our shared physical/spiritual experience. How can it be, other than in motion? Always in motion. And in that motion—as that motion—we are called away with it, forever "half-wild with loss."

Surely this is a pure instance of Stevens's famous notion "poetry as the cry of its occasion / Part of the res itself and not about it."

So any talk one may do about the shape and form and movement of this poem (and one should do much) should be about this complex of thought, should be about the isness of the poem, its physical presence in (and as) the world.

✳

A little earlier I said that we were not talking about clever poetic tricks, not about a mere crafty deftness by the poet. Of course by saying that I did not mean to suggest that such matters should not be considered. Rather, I was reminding us that the subject was/is something more important than that, something that eludes, finally, all attempts to codify and define. My purpose was to insist that all systems (of scansion, for instance) must be judged against the living complexity of poems, not the other way round. We need a more sensitive, a more flexible, a more subtle body of critical tools to talk to ourselves about prosody with.

Robert Hass speaks of poetry's reaching always for a more complex notion of form: not a reductive thinking, but an enlarging one, one that reaches out—in order to see more, to hold more: to be more. And it is that that we are interested in: not in final truths, not in absolutes about relative matters.

*

In his book *Men's Lives*, Peter Matthiessen writes of walking beside the ocean some years ago and seeing the skeletal head of a whale washed up on the beach on Long Island. He is excited by the event, and awed by it. For where once these great creatures were so plentiful they could be "taken" (meaning "killed" and brought to land) by small boats sent out from the nearby shore, they have long since been hunted to the edge of extinction (the right whale has almost disappeared from the planet) so that now even a skeleton is a rarity. There is of course something awesome about the size of this head he has found (old whalers there said it was the largest they had ever seen). But also awesome is the absence in it: the life gone out of it—and by implication out of the species, out of the planet even. For what Matthiessen is most aware of, as he looks at it and thinks about it, is the disappeared life: that miraculous event that comes and goes, comes and goes, its blue breath shining momentarily in the vast blackness of space.

But what size container does it need? Well, consider Robert Creeley's small poem "Echo":

> Back in time
> for supper
> when the lights

Can this be an instance of a successful attempt? Is life in its fullness actually present here—infinitely large, infinitely small?

I believe it is. What gives the poem its greatest claim on my trust, I think, is the utterly undefended indeterminacy of it: the way it interrupts silence for a moment, hardly more than an instant—and then only to make present the always-uncompleted quality of life in the present tense. (And of course that *is* the tense of life recalled, life remembered. When memory actually makes it present again, that is exactly what it is: present—everything pending once more, unresolved, in motion, the sweet poignance of expectation.) So there, in "Echo," it is: a tiny pinhole point of light in the dark wrapping of time; where again, for an eternal instant, childhood's trust and fear are called back; where the voices (of parents? of siblings?) call us back, to that timeless image of the rhythm of perfection: darkness comes, home's lights (come on), and the world continues. . . .

But of course this voice is so faint it is almost part of the silence itself, the silence we immediately fall back into, the incompletion of the moment forever embodied in the poem. Is it too much to say that the lights are both there and not there? I wouldn't want to get too precious about this, but the line "when the lights" strikes me as the simplest, and purest, sort of presentational gesture: one in which a statement about the lights is not made; it does not turn the corner and say "come on." But it does say the fact of lights, does announce them, so to speak. And the syntax of the mind, as well as the structure of experience, pulls us irresistibly to the next line, expecting to say "come on." But the line is missing. And even though we say "come on" soundlessly, still the words seem an invasion of the great silence that greets us there, the absence of the expected, the desired completion—one which time, perhaps inevitably, denies us.

I am touched by that endless suspension, the mortality its dreams are about.

✷

Consider this poem by Jane Miller:

BECAUSE YOU ARE FLESH

Birds wake the calves
who low a little, low a little.

Wind leafs through glass to my bed.
Waiting wakes me.

There's one light on the hillside,
yours, one story I'm interested in.

It's partly a telling, partly a becoming,
like mother having to be held and told,

so long since she's been a child.
A few good years spent

looking out
for accidents yield

details: a car is a fire coming closer.
Bulldogs and cattails swell the air.

Just when there's something,
like children we beg for it

to disappear. One morning
they're painting the rowboats blue

at Owl's Head. We glide the lake
too lovely to touch down,

like after an illness you have
sensitive hearing. Some days stand out

real or not.
Two bluebirds speck the heavens and move on.

The life in this poem is so intense I can hardly bear it. But
of course it is so intense I cannot look away from it either, even

for a moment; don't want to; cannot deny or resist its sensuous call, the world's deep-blue annunciation in the first two lines

> Birds wake the calves
> who low a little, low a little.

calling to me, calling to me, calling me into life. The world is present to me, I am in love with it, cannot love it enough—the ravishing music it makes. And as it moves steadily into its mystery—waking and sleeping, mother and child, the complex identities its pairings make—I am haunted by the power of its strange moments of seeing, life as a fever of feeling.

And then there's the way the small electrical short circuits play across many of the couplets, subverting for a moment the sentences' pull down the page of the mind and illuminating with their strange fire the visual moments of rest:

> looking out
> for accidents yield

This wonderful poem is all presence, the intensity of being. There is no clear "narrative" lying snugly back in there somewhere, where the truth can finally be ferreted out, if we're clever enough, or persistent enough. For narrative can't contain it, can't support all its complexity.

Few things are simply one thing or another. Ask any chemist. The syntax of reality is a complex one, and a poem must try to both see it and hear it. What's at stake is not just truth, but life. Because we are flesh, we are immersed in world transforming, the constant metamorphosis of memory and desire:

> Just when there's something,
> like children we beg for it

Yes, it's partly a telling and partly a becoming. It comes and it disappears. We beg for it, we hug it to ourselves, real or not, and it lifts us up. And because we are real, because we are flesh, it moves on.

✳

So much depends, of course, upon seeing the words in their becoming, upon seeing them become the physicality of the world. Seeing them become the aspects we must not look away from. The planes and surfaces and bodies we must not look away from. *Here we are, we are the pieces,* they remind us. *Look close and you will see us. Look close and you will see yourself: seeing.*

And of course hearing. Hearing the music of existence, the very tone and sound of it. Listen, for instance, to this haunting poem by Stanley Plumly.

SNOWING, SOMETIMES

You couldn't keep it out.
You could see it drifting
from one side of the road
to the other—you could watch
the wind work it back and forth
across the hard white surfaces.
You could see the maple, with
its ten dead leaves, winded,
wanting it. But sometimes
you couldn't keep it out.

It was like dust, an elegance,
like frost. All you had to
do was stand at the window
and it passed, like the light,
over your face—softer than light
at the edges, the seams,
the separations in the glass.
All you had to do was stand
still in the dark and the room
seemed alive with it, crystalline,
bright breath on the air.

If you fell asleep you knew
it could cover you, cover you
the way cold closes on water.

It would shine, like ice,
inside you. If you woke up
early, the cup on the bureau
cracked, you were sure that
even the pockets of your pants,
hung on the back of the chair,
would be filled. Nothing could
stop it, could keep it out.

Not the room in sunlight, nor
smoky with the rain. Not
the mother sweeping, nor
building the woodfire each
morning. Not the wind blowing
backwards, without sound.
Not the boy at the window
who loves the look of it
dusting the ground, whiter
than flour, piled in the

small, far corners.

Attend, oh attend, poems often seem to be saying to us, saying
to themselves: as with the French, *attendez*, meaning note, ob-
serve, pay attention, listen! Attend, oh attend.

You couldn't keep it out.
You could see it drifting
from one side of the road
to the other—you could watch
the wind work it back and forth
across the hard white surfaces.
You could see the maple, with
its ten dead leaves, winded,
wanting it. But sometimes
you couldn't keep it out.

Are these lines more involved in looking at the detail of
snowing, the details of the always local that snow falls on, or in

listening to it, listening to the words that allow it, the words that its mysterious presence occurs in? We wouldn't want to choose between them. We can't choose between them. It is, we feel, attending: attending to the very existence that snow here both enters and, in some compelling fashion, stands forth as. There is, of course, the sensual, physical presence of snow

> at the edges, the seams,
> the separations in the glass.

and of snow as activity, "drifting / from one side of the road / to the other." But equally present is the dreamlike quality of the voice we are hearing, the voice the poet is hearing—and being: the way it repeats and repeats, as in a dream, a trance almost, an unresisting fascination. *You could . . . you could . . . you could*, in the first stanza; *all you had to do, all you had to do*, in the second stanza: the snow emerging as a restless, insistent presence. And by implication, the fascinated passive presence of the observer. And again by implication: the almost spiritual presence, the living dimension of it:

> a bright breath on the air

Then, growing, snow as the detail of existence, the life one is waiting into, the drift that is both sleeping and waking.

> If you fell asleep you knew
> it would cover you, cover you

becoming, finally, in the fourth stanza, the insistent "nots":

> Not the room in sunlight, nor
> smoky with the rain. Not
> the mother sweeping, nor
> building the woodfire each
> morning. Not the wind blowing . . .

The simple inevitability of it. In these quotidian details—details of the elementally present life of the individual, denied and denied by the one-way movement of time, the unstoppable blow and drift and seep and whisper of the snow—in these details the absolutely full content of human existence is established: the inescapable, irresistible mortality that is always in it; the awfulness of it—filled with the awe of beauty and of loss and of light and of the movement everything exists as. In the vulnerability and innocence of childhood looking out, half in love with easeful death, we watch the detail of human existence drift and blow, drift and blow, as mysterious as breath, as dreams, as the words that place it before us, again and again: the dark and bright music they are together, snowing, sometimes.

"The movement everything exists as," I said a moment ago. And that seems to me a sound observation, maybe even an important one—for both physics and metaphysics. Also for aesthetics. The question "Where do we find the presence of aliveness in a poem, where do we look for it?" might reasonably be answered: where we find real movement, movement that is not merely superficial, but which implicates the presence of life experienced, "being" in the act of becoming. It is where literal and metaphorical are one, the conscious and unconscious life equally present in the moment of the poem.

> Not the wind blowing
> backwards, without sound.
> Not the boy at the window
> who loves the look of it
> dusting the ground, whiter
> than flour

The wind blowing forwards, blowing backwards: the immense complexity of our two-way existence in time; the mystery of it, absolutely present at this moment, "piled in the / / small, far corners."

Note: The poetry quotations on pages 23–24 are from, in order, Robert Bly, Charles Wright, William Carlos Williams, Walt Whitman, Walt Whitman, Emily Dickinson, and Wallace Stevens.

Notes on the Line

Poetry is carnal knowledge, the body—the world's body—actually present for a moment: on the page, in our ears, in our throats. Not the world as existent outside the poem, and to which the poem refers, but the world *in* the poem, the world *as* the poem. Language as the existent thing itself. Not just the mind's knowledge, but also the body's knowledge.

*

The body's knowledge, like the mind's, is complex, mysterious, obscure. But do we not, sleeping or waking, glimpse it in the "music" of our lives? touch it in the sounds we both make and hear?—in the silence we constantly break, and return to; in the shapes and motions our days and nights figure forth; in the involuntary rhythms we voluntarily enact.

This is the music that, living, we make. And it is both function, and measure, of the actuality of the world as we engage it, the music which, in poems, we become.

*

We have long been told that an iambic beat is the one most natural to the English language. And I do in part believe it. I remember someone even saying somewhere (I think it was Howard Nemerov) that he thought his very heartbeat was iambic. Powerful testimony. Still, I wonder about other possible rhythms our bodies know, the beats of our other organs. The slow tumble and roll of the gonads in their scrotal sac. The darker, slower rhythm the menses mark. The beats sensed, and responded to, inside the occipital cup, as the blood circulates along its long, familiar route and the lungs pump and pump us rhythmically toward the future, the medulla oblongata maintaining our delicate balance on the moving earth.

*

The line is an aspect of the "privileging" of art, a declaration that this is art, and therefore distinct (differentiated) from that which it sets itself off from. It draws attention to its form as visual fact, a visual declaration: *here, in this form, is the perception; here, seen and heard, is the complex music this (experience of the) world is.* The line (both in itself, and as part of a larger structure) is aspect and instrument of the difficult search a poem makes to accurately hear the music, and to make the experience bodily present.

For this to occur, I believe, the poet must, through memory and imagination, return to a condition of "being-in-the-world," *inter esse,* in the midst: back to an awareness of the living quality of an experience, an experience that in part was not and is not a conscious one.

There are several sources through which the unconscious content can be re-engaged, re-evoked: form (rhythm, sound, duration: the music) perhaps paramount among them.

To actually hear the music is, for the poet, to know the presence of fullness, experience irradiated by meaning.

*

Donald Barthelme has written that a fundamental difficulty for a writer is "the silencing of an existing rhetoric." He is speaking of the primary need to make oneself as free as possible of the confining thought patterns received rhetoric must of necessity impose. All "thoughts," Emerson suggests, are a kind of prison, for they impose, to some extent, prejudice, or ignorance, or the partiality of vogue and popular style and belief. Perhaps we should say, therefore, that a fundamental difficulty for the poet is the silencing of an existing music. Not really a radical statement, merely an acknowledgment of how difficult, and yet how crucial, it is to hear the complex music of our truest lives, poised a moment in time and space.

✳

The line as a unit of rhythm seen, within a larger unit of rhythm still coming into view: the pulse of being, passing.

✳

To hear the music. And somehow to make it visible: not through abstract, notational signs, but with the world itself in action across and down the pages of our bodies, recording, linearly, in Galway Kinnell's words, "music blooming with failure,"

> *The still undanced cadence of vanishing*

✳

The pauses a line enacts and describes, the silences its ends touch and point to—these too are part of the deeper rhythms the body lives, and dies, by.

✳

Of course the reader must also be able—and willing—to hear the music. If the poet hears and sees rhythms and structures that enact, that embody, the irrational, the discontinuous, the random, the irreconcilable, then the reader must not insist on hearing a music only of balance and symmetry and comfort.

*

In physics it has been found that deep inside the atom some events occur by chance. Is it possible that our bodies, deep in their own atomic tremble, trace the line of this knowledge anxiously across the durational space of our lives?

*

Western literature, like Western philosophy, as Heidegger has said, has been obsessed with endings, giving ontological priority to form over process, the whole over its parts. In short, obsessed with metaphysics.

Free verse, it seems to me, has been an attempt, at the level of the line, to break free from that obsession.

*

The line as "part of the res itself."

*

Overall, in this century, the movement has been toward increasing the dis-closive function of the line. Despite occasional lapses and in spite of a spate of poems whose lines read like the EKGs of Body Snatchers, the line has tended to respond to rhythm as internal form, form as epistemology. From the dart and pause of the eye and mind in the poems of William Carlos Williams—their energized movement, horizontally and vertically, together with the momentary arrest, the existent moment in space—from these to the long, richly layered lines we sometimes use today, continually opening out to further layers of loss and absence and celebration, the authentic poems of our time enact rhythms so accurate they make our bodies tremble with the knowledge, as in dreams. More importantly, they offer a fullness of the world in themselves. In the music they hear

and report, they are so full, have reinhabited a life so completely, that for a space one feels the poem is in touch with not
just *a* life but *the* life, the life we all as individual humans define
in ourselves. Thus in some of our most personal poems, our
most lyrical, I-centered moments, the poems seem to move us
into a larger—perhaps a deeper—sense of being. It is as if
somehow these events move into a significance nearer to that
of myth, where, in an instant of individual existence, the story
of the race is caught sight of.

Incarnations

In the beginning was the word: a recognition and a desire, a realization and a longing.

Words, we say, are a mode of being. Ourselves, we add, a mode of question.

      And so we come
             to the page

    again and again
           in quest

    hoping, seeking

    our eyes our ears our mouths
    shaped for existence,

    the ceaseless search the word

    life is

✳

To arrive disarmed except for language.
              – George Oppen

✳

To speak of the nature of poetry without, for some supposed convenience or ease of understanding, reducing it, requires that we speak in metaphor, that we *think* metaphorically. The attempt to speak of the very nature of poetry is an attempt to speak of what has, as an essential part of its being, something that reaches beyond reason's categories (so well articulated in Kant's critique of pure reason). Its beyondness, its transcendence, its sacredness, perhaps all this requires, finally, the exercise of the imagination. It requires that the objective world and the subjective world be a whole. It requires, in short, metaphor, which is the imagination's ability—the language's ability—to say both at once, the point where matter and meaning meet.

✳

Speech did not arise as the attempt of men to imitate, to master or explain 'Nature'; for speech and nature came into being along with one another. Strictly speaking, only idolators can raise the question of the origin of language. For anyone else to do so is like asking for the origin of origin. Roots are the echo of nature herself sounding in man. Or rather, they are the echo of what once sounded and fashioned in both of them at the same time.

              – Owen Barfield

✳

Question: What constitutes, for the poet, the call to a poem?

Answer: For me, it is the sense that what I am thinking/writing—the words in their flow and movement, their *shapely* emergence on the page—that this is not expressible by mere "writing." It has a music to it, a feel of movement and sound and tone that are, together, a presence, something that is, in a sense, independent of me, independent of postulation and argument and declaration.

We're trying to think here about art as a reaching, a reaching after a depth that is in us, after what Thoreau calls "that secret life" each of us has within.

These are the key words: *attempt, search*—perhaps *find*.

✷

I once read an assessment of a poet's work in which the critic complained that the poetry did not show "a strong use of metaphor." But of course poetry is not about the *use* of metaphor. It is about—or committed to—the *exploration* for metaphor, about the *finding* of metaphor, about the *being* of metaphor: not metaphor as invention, of course, or even as tool, but metaphor as recognition, as seeing, as *dis*covery. To the extent that a poem *is* something; to the extent that it actually embodies its meaning and its existence: to that extent, the poem *is* metaphor.

"That which exists through itself," Charles Olson writes, "is what we call meaning."

✷

What the work "knows" arises in large part from unconscious sources and is often expressed in and through the formal qualities of the work. In a poem, for instance, this "knowledge," this "knowing," is to a great extent revealed (to both poet and reader) through the music of the poem—its rhythms, its combination of sounds, its tempos, its silences. This music seems to express a knowledge, an awareness, which the psyche's corporeal involvement has most direct access to. It's an awareness we say affects us "deeply," the metaphor suggesting our perception that these aspects of the work reach us through avenues other than consciousness.

This capacity of the "form" of a poem to bear and embody "meaning" is of course not a simple matter. And to adequately investigate or even identify its many aspects would lead us into consideration of visual as well as auditory patterns and shapes. It would require us to consider what the eye, as well as the ear, provides us—the music we "see" as well as that we hear. And it would require that we consider the actual shape(s) the poem assumes on the page: as meaning, as source; e.g., the length of individual lines, the grouping of lines, the visual tensions within and between groupings, even the role of white space, that visual silence the poem speaks into. ("Significant speech," Heidegger reminds us, unlike idle chatter, breaks the silence only in order to call attention to something greater.)

In considering these matters, many poets have been drawn to a recognition of the *physical* presence of the poem—its very body—as seat and site of the struggle for "seeing" that serious art strives for: the struggle to "see" something whole, to see it as, if only for an instant, enduring, something one participates in, something existent beyond one's power to define it. They have found the poem to be, not a report on something (either an "external" world or thoughts *about* such a world), but rather itself a participant in the struggle.

"Not ideas about the thing," writes Stevens, "but the thing itself."

✳

The impulse to art comes, not from a desire to control being, but from a longing to be at one with it, the holy unity of it. "Be it life or death, it is reality we are after," Thoreau says. Yes, we say, and add: Life *and* death, it is being we are after.

✳

. . . Recognizing the complex life words lead, as both subjects and objects, the unconscious life of the body released, for a space, into awareness . . .

"The poet also uses the word," Heidegger says, "not, however, like ordinary speakers and writers, who have to use [words] up, but rather in such a way that the word only now becomes and remains truly a word."

✳

A poetry denies its end in any descriptive act, I mean an act which leaves the attention outside the poem.

— Robert Creeley

✳

The page: as locus for the music of Being to be seen (and heard) in.

The page: where we have the opportunity to see words as living presences, as existential facts, not just as signs pointing toward an "external" reality.

The page: where we have the opportunity to avoid destroying a word by its associations.

✳

The fact that a poem does not "refer" to a reality outside itself, that it does not "point," does not mean that, its gaze being fixed clearly on the page, it is about itself instead of about the world. Rather, it means that the physical fact of the poem—the words as physical events, the lines and the grouping of lines, the shapes and patterns, both visual and auditory, which develop *on the page*—all this is inextricably entangled in the reality that the poem both explores and is. This, it seems to me, is simply so, whether the poet is "aware" of it or not, whether he makes use of this knowledge or not. What the poet "knows" is product of this complex interaction. And the poem *is* its seeing.

For us, in our time, there can be no going back from this understanding of the art, this awareness of the phenomenological complexity of it. There can be only evasion, or the inattention of insincerity—and a resultant poetry about which we might say, with Williams, "There is not life in the stuff because it tries to be 'like' life."

   ✳

The dynamic of the page: where we encounter words alive in the forcefield of existence, their hair blown back, their eyes tearing from the wind.

   ✳

The substance, the means, of an art, is an incarnation—not reference but phenomenon.

– Denise Levertov

   ✳

> Say it's a spill of acorns
> in the trail, each curved edge a line
>
> between light and shade
> the ground grows solid
>
> by: *oh let not*
> *any absence fall*
>
> we seem to hear the voice of air
> around us saying
>
> *between this full moment*
>
> *and the next* and already the brush
> is starting its thick pull
>
> of presence
> across our life, the eternal the moment
> swells into
>
> existence as, contingency
> forever shaped
>
> in sight: the wind
> that sweeps all day

the leaves, the water
that reflects
off its dark body

light
everything that is
curves into color

through: here
trees can still

be seen, that mysterious
respiration matter

comes steadily and steadily
to mind as

✳

One cannot "make it up" completely. One cannot find, in the fancy, something to substitute for the world of primary experience. We cannot, like the God in *Green Pastures*, say, "Give me some more firmament," and then with that primal matter mold forth the image in our minds. The only firmament we can apprehend is that which, through the moment of perception, we participate in the existence of.

✳

Thus for me nature is never a convention. I am interested, as man and as artist, in nature as environment, as embodiment, as process—and in respect to art, especially as process. Nature, it seems to me, *is* the process. Or rather, it is *the* process—whether one is thinking about the mind (its own "nature," its working) or about the way the world continues: how it lives and dies and lives. And my major clue is "nature," the phenomenal world, the *inhabited* planet, that complex organism we both see and are. What I seek to do in my art is to provide an opportunity for it to show itself—body and breath—in living enactment of its process, its constant move in and through being—

words launched from treetop
nests miraculous

with meaning

*

Tone is not some quality the poet is able to "put into" the poem. It is, rather, the presence of reality "known": the individual, experiencing psyche knowing an environment, the poem knowing an environment. Sincerity demands it, can't (or won't) proceed without it. It is presence; it is authority; it is reciprocal trust—or sincerity—perceived.

*

The poem is, for me, not just the world appearing *to* itself, but also the world appearing *as* itself, the being *and* the becoming, process and event as one, subatomic reality structuring itself in and as mind: in short, "the phenomenal world," which is what *we* call nature, and which I look on constantly in love and astonishment and awe and dread and exaltation.

When one speaks of poetry as process (as some have eloquently done), these, I believe, are some of the important implications of the idea. To be sure, all writing is a process. But that simple fact is not what is implied by the term here, not at any significant level. Rather, what is pointed to is the poem's participation in being, in the self-existent world, whose structure, whatever it is, is the poem's structure, for it is the only *meaningful* one. "The work of the imagination," says Williams, "is not 'like' anything but [is] transfused with the same forces which transfuse the earth." And elsewhere: "Invention of new forms to embody this reality of art, the one thing which art is, must occupy all serious minds concerned."

We are speaking here, it seems to me, of the necessity for form to have epistemological function. For again come the basic questions: How does the poem—how does the poet—know what the poem knows? How can we believe it? How can the poet believe it? What is the source? What is its reality? Is it, in fact, *meaning*? Intention and will and ego have very little to do, ultimately, with the answers to these important, these basic, questions. Humility, sincerity, openness—these have to do with them. The unconscious has to do with them. Rocks and trees and dreams and the snorts of beasts have to do with them. And perhaps virtue. "Virtue of the mind is that emotion which causes to see," George Oppen says. And of course it is the "to see" that is usually absent, whether we're speaking of poetry or of politics. I am always trying to turn my face in the direction whence might come seeing. And a poem—to the extent that it exists through itself, to the extent that it is itself the world becoming, always, itself/ourself, its body *completely at one with* the process through which we die and yet give off light—this, for me, is the principal moment of seeing, the timeless moment of verbal insight.

❋

To be receptive. Learning to listen, and to see. Attending. Being open to the phenomena and their content.

It is a sincere regard for the poem, as moment of being's occurrence, that determines that the poet will be in a position to discover—to know—through the poem.

❋

Classical form, John Cage said, has to do with *concept* and its understanding. The music we are committed to must have to do, first, with *perception* and its arousal.

Learning to recognize, for example, the syntax of silence.

Its role can be witnessed not only in poetry but also in music and painting, even in dance. Consider how in Merce Cunningham's choreography, for example, stasis and absence and silence step forward onto the stage and take their place as equals in the developing patterns life bodies forth there, the numen seen a moment in these pairings and pauses: both the self, and the other.

✳

. . . Trying to think of prosody as linkage between the spoken and the unspoken, bringing into the poem some of the presence of the unspoken: silence as reality larger than language can account for . . .

✳

If, as Heidegger says, what a poem has to set into itself is being, then obviously "being" means more than "intention" or "meaning" or "idea" or "concept" or any other term that refers to or identifies some aspect, or even the whole, of pure consciousness and reason.

Art, says Magritte, "evokes the mystery without which the world would not exist."

✳

Seeking connections, intuiting the unity . . .

There is a vast difference between "I have something to say" and "There is something that needs to be said." The former is like going into the woods with a gun. All the wild words run away and hide in the earth's secret places. The best you can hope for is to see a track.

✳

. . . Rhythm as internal form, part of the pulse and energy of the phenomenal world, which we must always turn toward, not only as meaning and metaphor, but as existence . . .

✳

We must talk of music, of the poem's voice as it makes available its content. And we must talk of the physically appearing facts of the poem's existence. Its lines: their movements and their associational discoveries; their linguistic articulation of being's transformations, as it makes itself available to us and constantly withdraws itself, an agon of forever resisting and being over-come. Here we are thinking of language making itself available to our sight as well as to our hearing. Language seen, Being seen: in the spaces we clear out for it on the page, in the openings the poem is always becoming for it to be present in.

✳

To see
as well as hear it,
somehow to see

the music happen,
as when moonlight lies down
each night in the shallow graves

of footprints, that faint
hint of bones
in the outlines light

scribes across whatever page our life
faces up to, notes
we leave for ourselves

everywhere we turn:
With human beings,
Rilke says, we are in the habit of learning much

from their hands, and everything
from their face, there where light catches
a moment and shapes

some precinct of
trees rocks water
words, the face

of the world
we take in our hands, lines
we make in the air

to describe its presence,
the long sift of darkness into our mouths
as song

＊

It is man's sincerity and depth of vision that makes him a poet. See deep
enough, and you see musically; the heart of Nature being everywhere
music, if you can only reach it.

— Thomas Carlyle

＊

As respects poetry's ability to sound the world's living presence,
to sense and inhabit its vital movement in time and space, its
body manifest, one might say, echoing Emily Dickinson, "I sing
a music never schemed." Perhaps one could say "a music never
scanned" and still be accurate, the point being that "systems" of
scansion would always be inadequate to a *complete* description
of the music. But "never schemed" carries perhaps the addi-
tional force of the music's having been released into its fullest
possibilities of discovery, its freedom from conceptual restric-
tions of what is either possible or acceptable.

＊

If one of the primary qualities of poetry is "to offer up the
world again," freed of preconceptions and preconditions, res-
cued from declarative partiality, then surely one of the poet's
primary needs—even an ethical responsibility—is to allow the
poem to hear and embody—*to incarnate*—the experience's truest music, the world's music. What greater enemy to such freedom than the "idolatry" of some privileged forms?

＊

Yet what does form mean? I do not even know what it means to ask the
question. All I know is that when I ask it, I am in the existential world
and that it can only be answered there. The answer may, in fact, be the
existential world.

— Carl Rakosi

＊

"Negative capability," says Keats, "that is, when a man is capable of being in uncertainties, mysteries, doubts, without any
irritable reaching after fact and reason—Coleridge, for instance, would let go-by a fine isolated verisimilitude caught
from the Penetralium of mystery, from being incapable of remaining content with half-knowledge."

What Keats terms negative capability is the capacity to resist the
conscious mind's almost irresistible drive to understand, to define, to categorize, to explain. The capacity he is speaking of is
the opposite of what we call "scientific" thought, the opposite
of the drive to abstraction. Negative capability identifies, in
other words, the *participatory* capacity of mind, not the explanatory, the judgmental, the form-giving.

＊

Form, says Valéry, is costly.

＊

Every sincere poem is an enactment of its epistemology. *It* is
how one knows that what one writes is sincere, honest, true. It
is the presence of, at once, both its uncertainty and its moment
of knowing. As Heidegger puts it, "Each answer remains in
force only as long as it is rooted in questioning." The poet must
feel and believe that the work of art, the poem, is what makes
available its content and at the same time tests it for truth. The
weakness of most poetry of assertion is its arrogance, its hubris,
its cock-sureness, which proceeds from the poet's assumption
of some extra-artistic, some extra-existential source of knowing. Sincerity, on the other hand, requires an openness to an
arriving of truth. Perhaps a primary importance of Williams's
familiar declaration "no ideas but in things" is its insistence on
the poem as epistemological event: the poem both contains and
is the things which embody its "ideas." The poets must always
challenge what they see or utter, must demand that it prove
itself *to them*. They can never accept what has not been made

present in the work, its insistent encounter and re-encounter of the physical world on the page, its sensuous touch and touch. . . .

*

The word happens to us; we suffer it, for we are victims of a profound uncertainty.

– C. G. Jung

*

Reticence and sincerity: a necessary pairing. They represent and make possible a sensitivity to authentic speech, with its pressure of the unspoken, the unsayable.

To see the thing coming into being, the *gestalt* it makes—always opening and withdrawing—the figure this unique moment of being, in its momentariness, is visible in.

*

Consider another possibility of meaning for "free" in the term "free verse": namely, as a "liberating," a freeing up: of the imagination, of one's seeing, of one's powers of *in*sight; a way of releasing, perhaps, some of the bonds of pure rationality, removing some of its props: all those verse conventions, for example, that fix and define, that declare and posit. Further, it seems to invoke (by extension) the possibility of a formal exploration that moves farther and farther away from the stays against insight that the conventional forms of declarative writing provide: punctuation, unequivocal syntax, even, at times, the sentence itself—its dispositions of certainty. . . .

*

The dynamic of the page: the developing physical "presence" in the words and their combinations: the sounds they make in their movement, the shapes they assume there.

The dynamic of the page: the "field" in which discovery is worked out, the scene we glimpse it in.

The dynamic of the page: where we catch sight of the phenomenon that is the poem.

*

. . . Lines as a dialectic between individual words and the syntax of larger utterance, a dialectic that exists simultaneously as visual, as temporal, as conceptual occurrence: a dialectic that exists both in and across the lines.

*

Consider how in the poetry of open forms it is possible for the verse to capture the very act of world transforming, thought's syntax entangled in the lines' embodiment of object *becoming* that larger complex, that fuller complex, which is metaphor: matter becoming spirit, earth becoming world. It is existence presenced, the always existential moment released into awareness.

Writing in open forms means being alert to developing possibilities, learning to recognize other sources of order and meaning and pattern than ego and will.

The desire to see what happens happen . . .

*

So much depends, of course, upon seeing the words in their becoming, upon seeing them *become* the physicality of the world. Seeing them become the aspects we must not look away from. The planes and surfaces and bodies we must not look away from. *Here we are, we are the pieces*, they remind us. *Look close and you will see us. Look close and you will see yourself: seeing.*

*

Open form does not yield to an easy rationalist division of meaning, is not reducible to familiar and unambiguous distinctions and patterns. It is not easily codifiable—if at all. The very language one uses to describe it seems at times to be a language that alters familiar views of language, to be a language that preserves rather than resolves questions, one that leads us into further complication rather than into resolution.

✳

The spirit that has been driving poetry (and art in general) to open forms in this century expresses a world that, in physics, required that we devise the theory of quantum mechanics. It is a spirit that eludes the finality of strict forms, one that cannot be expressed in the certainties those formal patterns require and express. Like quantum mechanics, which deals only in probabilities, it is neither neat nor predictable. It is a spirit that demands that serious artists refuse Newtonian simplifications. We are all familiar with the story William Carlos Williams tells in his autobiography of the painter who, when asked by a potential buyer to identify something near one corner of the canvas, studied it carefully a few minutes before replying that he did believe, Madam, that was paint. It's a funny story. But it also points clearly to one of the most important developments in art and mind in our century: namely, the recognition that one fact as true (and perhaps as important) as any other about a painting, a work of art, is that it is made up of materials which have undeniable physical existence, not only prior to the work of art but also *as aspect of* the work of art. The paint. The canvas. Colors. Textures. Space—both empty and filled. In a poem, the page: the actual physical presence of the page itself. And so the visual fact of the words and lines upon it. Their appearance there. Their life there. From this germ can be derived an entire body of thought about art, not as a simple representation of some "out there," some certainty, some declarable "objective" reality known somehow by a process of apprehension and thought which the painting itself is not an essential part of; but rather art as polarity, as conversation: logos appearing to itself.

✳

Not a *trompe l'oeil* facsimile, but matter itself. Quiddity. The world's body seen. The word's body said.

✳

In poetry, the work of poets such as William Carlos Williams, George Oppen, Charles Olson, Robert Creeley, Denise Levertov, A. R. Ammons—to name a few—was always an attempt to explore the implications of these ideas, these facts. Through the work of these and countless other artists, we came to sense, however uncertainly, something of the Doppler effect that came from the light-speed rush away from us of anything resembling a purely "objective" reality. We came, over time, to *feel* the reality of this shift: in focus, in awareness. Came to take it for granted; but also came finally, many of us, to see these profound grapples with reality as no more than matters of "style," as if they could be detached from their complex aesthetic-intellectual ground of experience, and put on and taken off like clothing: matters of mere fashion.

✳

> *The question is: how does one hold an apple*
> *Who likes apples*
>
> *And how does one handle*
> *Filth? The question is*
>
> *How does one hold something*
> *In the mind which he intends*
>
> *To grasp and how does the salesman*
> *Hold a bauble he intends*
>
> *To sell? The question is*
> *When will there not be a hundred*
>
> *Poets who mistake that gesture*
> *For a style.*
>
>   – George Oppen

✳

What is occurring in recent arguments over the role and importance of traditional English poetic forms is not simply a new outbreak of the battle of the ancients and the moderns, updated from the seventeenth century. The problem is oversimplification. In a time when the technocrats rule our world and, increasingly, our lives, even the formal elements of poetry have come to be approached and pursued as *technical* elements. Thus in the last fifteen years or so the elements of free verse have all too often come to be employed as if the questions were mere technical questions. And free verse has tended, in the hands of those without vision or true imagination, to lose its essential connection to what is mysterious, what is beyond numeration or rational definition. ("An artist who paints without imagination," said the American painter George Henri, "is a mere mechanic.") It has become performance rather than embodiment, the poem as presentation rather than as place and act of discovery, the place and moment where, in Heidegger's terms, the world worlds. Unfortunately, what the new emphasis on "traditional" metrics does, in its reaction, is simply to accept this oversimplification. Those who are calling for a "return" to metrics as a "solution" are in fact calling for a *technical* solution, a nonartistic solution, and also of course for an oversimplified perception of the *artistic* problem.

✳

What we miss in work that is imitation rather than creation is the real presence of risk, the dare of failure, what Francis Ponge has called the "fumblings of Creation." We miss the risk of error, the grope to discovery from which might come the "happy creations" World is: work that actually participates in Creation's search, its "positive errors"; work that embodies the eternal poignance of time.

Desideratum: to achieve, in the work, a coincidence of opposites, the always-contingent quality of present tense, and, simultaneously, the sense of the eternal: the feeling of both at the same time—not just in the whole, but in every part as well. This is the challenge of art.

✴

I think that we (poets and readers alike) have been truly aware, or at least conscious, of only a small portion of what has been implicated in this century's explorations with open forms in art (including of course what is commonly called free verse). In poetry especially, I believe, our articulated theory has fallen far behind, has lost contact with the important questions about the nature of reality that poetry and all art must face, questions about the very nature of poetry, questions that are inextricably bound up with our understanding of the reality of the universe we live, and die, in: questions about form, about what form really "means," and about what sorts of relationship poetry's form has to matter itself, as well as to thought. The problem is that, with the exception of the original and searching writings of at best a double-handful of people (mostly poets), there has been up to now no truly public body of critical/theoretical thought that expresses the complexity of our best thinking about our world.

The most difficult problem . . . concerning the use of the language arises in quantum theory. Here we have at first no simple guide for correlating the mathematical symbols with concepts of ordinary languages. The only thing we know from the start is the fact that our common concepts cannot be applied to the structures of the atoms. . . . Even in large dimensions there are many solutions of the quantum-theoretical equations to which no analogous solutions can be found in classical physics. . . . It must be observed that the system which is treated by the methods of quantum mechanics is in fact a part of a much bigger system (eventually the whole world); it is interacting with this bigger system: and one must add that the microscopic properties of the bigger system are (at least to a large extent) unknown.

– Werner Heisenberg

✴

One fundamental question we need to address, it seems to me, is this: "To what extent can poetry, today, be sounded into the air?" How fully can we "say" it aloud? The question is, in a sense, "Does the pattern of sounds that the words and lines on the page invoke, and which one can theoretically render fully with the voice—does this pattern, this utterance, express fully the poem?"

Many other questions follow on this one. For instance, to what extent is poetry, for us, still essentially an orally based art form? The growth of poetry readings of the past twenty-five years would appear, on the face of it, to suggest that the answer might be unequivocal. But there are other questions as well, complicating questions: For example, to what extent can we *hear* most lines in contemporary poetry; that is, to what extent can we hear them as *lines*? How fully do traditional systems of sound in poetry express our sense of the rich music of most of the twentieth-century poems we love? How fully do they express the music of the logos in the late twentieth century, the word "man" overwhelmed by the vast noise of meaning-lessness?

And is there perhaps a music we can only see?

✳

My own sense is that, whether we are aware of it or not, the one-to-one relationship between the poem we see and the poem we say is as lost to us today as Newtonian mechanics. For Milton, I would guess, it was still possible, despite the fact that he was perhaps the world's most literate man in an already literate age, to give voice to practically 100 percent of the poetry in the poems he composed—and not only after he was blind and dictating to an amanuensis. The patterns of his poetry and of that of his contemporaries—with very few exceptions—were the patterns of sound only, the patterns of a prosody that existed independently of the page, that had no fundamental connection with the visual.

Today there are still attempts being made to reclaim that lost harmony, to write the poetry of a time before the certainties of either physics or prosody were replaced by probabilities. Even the present's new love affair with "narrative" poetry would seem to be a further expression of that attempt, that longing, with its emphasis on journalistic reporting's supposed capacity to tell "what really happened," to report, in short, a verifiable and objective reality.

✳

I find the work of many poets today uninteresting on the page, uninteresting to *read*, though not, necessarily, to listen to. Reading their work I feel as if the poet is not aware enough somehow, not attentive enough to the occurring moments the poem is. More than that, that the poet's allegiance lies outside the poem, that it is given to a "truth" the poem *refers* to, to one it *assumes* rather than to one it is. Which is perhaps simply a definition of insincerity.

The ancient and fortified city of Propaganda is only a short drive from here by car.

✳

Does this allegiance, I wonder, have anything to do with a "comfort" factor? In other words, is the poem less disturbing, less dislocational, less jarring, if it *can* be entirely heard? if syntax and an "objective" reality enclose it completely in familiar structure? Do reasserted allegiances to "English" ("traditional," "closed," "received") forms reflect, to some extent, nostalgia— a longing for the resolved, the nonconditional? an escape from indeterminacy, from contingency? from the "I-could-be-wrong"-ness existence's present-tense life always dwells in?

One thing that would seem to be missing there is a recognition of the role of the visual-spatial dimension of poetry—as aspect of relativity's complication of time, and space: its complication of that simple linear march of rhythms from one point to another, of the sounds those rhythms sing aloud from some (supposed) beginning to the (willed) end.

✸

What form is to the conventional mind is just what can be imposed, the rest is thought of as lacking in form.

– Robert Duncan

✸

Light. Space. The visible. Form *seen*.

Is not this experiential knowledge of self and world primal?—wherein shapes and patterns first enter us as living knowledge. Is not the bright presence of light there like milk the spirit drinks in as visual form?—shapes that loom and then disappear, that curve into food and also into warmth; shapes that take, and then bring back, the light; the darkness heads bend down from the sky into . . .

✸

> *And twofold Always. May*
> *God us keep*
> *From Single vision and Newton's*
> *Sleep!*
> — William Blake

✸

The question for art is always, it seems to me, how to make the moment existential, how to make it *living moment of the world*. It is in response to this challenge that free verse, or open form, appears to have made its most significant contribution in our time. Consider how free verse poems are able to isolate, identify, and release the infinite series of particularity matter exists as, its constant bloom into awareness.

Consider how, in its spatial indwelling on the page, the poem of open form has the opportunity to empower the white space, to invoke its participation in the unvoiced content of existence, that silent presence of being which can chasten the ego's willful and reckless rush into words.

Consider how, in this space, it is possible, just possible, that the poet, writing with sincerity and reverence and trust, might actually see, with his lines, the small human families of words, adrift forever in the great ocean of time.

> *There was no light at all every time*
> *an oil drum exploded*
> *the ground shook huge pillars*
> *of smoke went up they broke*
>
> *into a run they ran*
> *a few feet then went back*
> *to their dead walk*
> *their eyes closed*
>
> .　　.　　.　　.
>
> *like walking ghosts their arms*
> *bent forward like this*
> *they had a special way of walking—*
> *very slowly—like this—*
> 　　　　　– Marc Kaminsky, "them"

✳

Writing a poem—the act of writing a poem, the very process itself—seems to me something like groping along the membrane that separates, and joins, the material world and the mind. It is instance, somehow, of thinking seen. To me this is the most fundamental, the most searching form of thought. Through it—as it—mind and matter join: they define each other and become the whole which, as world, they are. And in this process, words seem to me to be released again into a fundamental individuality of existence, an existence as individuals possessed of an integrity that is both physical and spiritual. As the lines of the poem come into being on the page, as together

we struggle to make room and ground for this emergence—
the words in their own individual shapes as well as those shapes
which, in their emergence into sight and sound, they become
together—they reach out to me the feeling of life, the sense of
being itself, which we know we share. Through them, becoming the poem, I feel myself enter the wonder and poignance of
the present tense of the world, the emergence of being every
instant into life. At these moments—these timeless, durational
moments—the poem *is* the reality. In it I "see." For in it—*as
it*—the world emerges into a clarity and wholeness that invali-
dates discursive separations of "appearance" and "meaning,"
of "form" and "content," of "conscious" and "unconscious," of
"I" and "it." Here, in the poem—if I look sincerely/trustingly/
searchingly/uncompromisingly at the form-al emergence into
awareness that the-material-world-as-mind and mind-as-the-
material-world make together—it is possible to escape the partiality that the merely conscious mind imposes, the limiting
picture the ego/will presents to my awareness. I can, in short,
enter the sense of simultaneous awe and belonging that the
world is apprehended as. And I can enter it as moment of il-
lumination, as a literally timeless awareness, the durational
sense of the eternally temporal. The sense of *being in.* The
sense of *knowing as.* In this activity, this process, something like
an absolute balance is achieved, it seems to me, by looking, always, at the point where they truly meet: the poem on the
page. Literally *on* the page: its *visual* presence, the white silence
which the words enter bodily, and so take their places in an
emerging form they have life in. With them, on the page, we
enter actions and associations we only partly understand; but
whatever their meaning, whatever their signification, they are,
we feel, existence entered. In these lines, in their always contin-
gent groupings together, we can feel the actual pull of existence, the risk being takes at every moment as it continually
enters the great adventure of time.

And Now a Few Words

But I say unto you, that every idle word that men speak, they shall give account thereof in the day of judgment. For by thy words thou shalt be justified, and by thy words thou shalt be condemned.

Poetry, it seems to me, is always, in its very essence, an exploration of language: I mean an engagement of its very nature, a venture into the depths of its being. Most of today's thinking about language, the basis of most experimental and speculative thinking about it, proceeds from the notion that language is a system of signs, whose purpose and entire reason for being is communication. I believe such thinking ignores what is perhaps the most fundamental fact about language: that it is a creator, a creator of our humanness—perhaps *the* creator of our humanness.

It is language that ushers us into the world of human beings. By virtue of being individual humans we live, as Charles Simic says, in "two worlds at once, / one of which is unsayable." And it is language that puts us into that double world. It is language that creates us as inhabitants of that world. By the time a human child—genetically prepared for such creation—by the time that child begins to speak, it has already begun to participate in that double creation: being created by language, creating (self) with language. It has entered the double world, the metaphoric world, of human existence, the world that at all times both *is* and *means*, the world of finitude and infinity, of temporality and eternity. Perhaps we can never, as Simic says, say the "other." But it is of course language's very nature to participate in that otherness: to evoke it, to point to it, to long for it. It is language that makes us know that it exists. It is language that makes us know we are in it, that we are of it. Language is both means and cause of our doubleness. Through it we think infinity. As it, we long for eternity, one pole of our being always fixed in temporality's unceasing flow. Language is the creator of our being as humans. And that being exists always in two worlds at once.

Poetry is language's attempt—our attempt—to say that unsayable world. It is language's attempt to make our humanness fully present, its metaphoric mystery revealed. Not solved, or simplified, or explained, but revealed. Again and again and again. Poem after poem after poem—the spirituality of the world enabled to be perceived physically: life metaphoric. Is it not poetry's job to see and reveal this essence of language, this essence of human life, of life as human? Is that not language's challenge to itself, its constant urge to realization?

And always, at its core, the doubleness. Both the gulf and the reach. Both the knowing and the not-knowing. Both the world of forms—which we love and touch and name and hold to ourselves with adoration and with passion—and the always unsatisfiable longing, ourselves sheathed in a skin of time, through which we come together and fall apart, become visible and then vanish from sight. Always the I and the not-I, the poles between which this mysterious force of language flows, bathing all human experience in light and dark: both the sayable and the unsayable at once, that inescapable dialectic. This is language existential—its paradoxical life in the world, its essential life in the world. Our human life in the world.

*

I think one could say that art is always defining itself. Not in the sense of redefining, but rather in the sense of continuing to define—offering further possibilities of recognition, but each new recognition always only another figure glimpsed fleetingly in the mist, gone almost as we look at it. Still, the image—the moment—haunts us. We wake at night and see it again

> in the dark
>
> of our minds, the drift
> and sudden rise
>
> into memory . . .

One way of defining poetry, it seems to me, is to say that it is an attempt *to allow* the mystery of words—not just language, that familiar and tamed idea we have lived with for so long that we have come to take for granted the mysterious thing it identifies—like trees, like blue—but words themselves. To say, that is, that poetry provides (discovers? admits? experiences?) a context which allows the mystery of words to enact itself before our very eyes. Before their very eyes.

This definition—this action—is one which is particularly important in our time. Increasingly today people find it difficult to discover a means for thinking seriously about their own lives, difficult to find a direction to look in. So many beliefs swept away. So many perceptions called into question. Thus, pulled variously by the claims of taste, or dogma, or nostalgia, or cynicism, the mind itself is reduced to thought as fibrillation. A dangerous condition.

But in poetry words get released again into their own custody, so to speak, and so regain the power to discover perceptions and shapes and patterns that touch the rhythms of thought and feeling, patterns in which might be glimpsed, perhaps, the DNA of the psyche; even, perhaps, the quarks of the soul.

In poems, words inhabit again their existence as selves: yours, mine, theirs. In the poems' musical lines, words seem to hear themselves, singing. They seem to see themselves, speaking. It's where mind can feel itself, thinking.

In poems I hear my own body breathing in the words. When I hear them on the page—and in my throat and my chest and my hands—the music of them astonishes me, the undeniable authority of life, embodied. When I see them on the page, their bodies fill me with that mixture of desire and reverence which being, in its rich unfolding of life, makes available to itself as objects of love and despair. The poems return to me, in my always present entanglement in time, words as existence, words as sharers, words as glimpses of our selves, their searching touch along the bodies of thought we are constantly becoming.

✴

"Great poetry," Owen Barfield says, "is the progressive incarnation of life in consciousness." To the extent that it is great, Barfield seems to be pointing out, poetry is the thing actually achieved—seen and known: the true incarnation. Incarnate in consciousness itself.

By further implication, it seems to me, poetry (without, perhaps, the great) is here recognized to be the achieving, the actual coming into being. Perhaps we could say that the poem is being's conversation with itself: being appearing to itself. Also as itself.

Likewise, the poem is, I would suggest, one's conversation with the Other. As Merleau-Ponty says, "Speech and understanding are moments in the unified system of self-other." This "unified system of self-other" is the ground in which being confronts itself as both object and subject, existence and consciousness. It is also the arena of art.

And it is the arena of language. For it is as language, always coming into consciousness, that being carries on its conversation with itself. It is how mind carries on its conversation with the Other.

This is, of course, language as creator. When it enters us (with its memories, its associations, its internal necessities, its formal shapes and sounds and densities), the timelessness of words enters Time: all the ancestral coding of our spirit-bodies stirs our tongues, sings out again our endless mortal longing, the articulation of our desire.

*

"Did I pray when I was forming pots?" says Elizabeth White, a Hopi potter. "Absolutely. The clay is a living being. When you put it in your hand . . . look at it: a lump . . . a lump that says to me, Make me as I am . . . Make me beautiful. So we converse every step of the way, the clay and I."

*

Desire. Its constant recognition of separation. Its always longing for reattachment. Its longing toward the Other, in which it sees itself—completed. Its hunger for the appearances, the bodies it becomes. "Our deepest desire," says Galway Kinnell, "is to be one with all creation."

To be at one with. To be at home.

This is also language as *logos*, as *nous*; the word as ultimate metaphor: Take this body of mine into your mouth, it is my beloved. Metaphor, as Gaston Bachelard wrote, is an instant metaphysics.

And of course this is language as our existential condition. It is the life of being. The life of Life. The sacred gift of language experienced as the voice of the world, which utters us into the realm of being.

As poetry, it is existence singing.

*

Some such experience seems to be involved in my own obsessions in the poetry I write—the way in which I am obsessed by the music of it, its insistent call to me, the mysterious power it seems to come from. That wondrous sense of merging, of being realized: the voice of spirit as matter, their verbal conjugation. Paradoxically, the visual dimension of the poems on the page is fundamental to my experience of their form, part of their very DNA; but all the movement, all the pulse and breath of them, is in and as music, its sacramental utterance. My allegiance to it, the utterly primary role of it in the imagination's search for form, seems completely involuntary. And inescapable. I dwell on and in it in the making, set my uncertain course by it. And I feel that the poetry is the only means by which I can, at present, seriously encounter and inhabit—in my own work—the essential grope and quest and prayer that poetry is. The only way I can find something I can trust, something I can believe; the only avenue to some kind of essentiality—the blue planet as life's own breath and body, awhirl and adrift in vastness, singing the morning song of rising, the evening song of setting, and calling its lovely/lonely names out into the endless waiting, the listening we exist as.

And the Look of the Bay Mare

Shames Silliness Out of Me

In poetry, free verse has clearly been the lingua franca of our time. That is to say, the forms that "modernism" and "postmodernism" found out and created have become our traditional forms. They are the forms our poems think with, the rhythms they feel in. And not just as some sort of Esperanto, unable in its simplicity ever to touch the true genius of any language. On the contrary, it is a language that is personal and local. And in America, at least, this is a language that is personal and local to us. What we hear in it is the music of the land, and the words we say it with. Or the words we are used to say it by.

And to me this language is beautiful, with the purity and freshness that only language at one with the world it speaks for can be: its rhythms, its colorings, its sense of time and place. Part of the strength of free verse, I suspect, resides in its capacity to be local—and at the same time universal. Czeslaw Milosz has said that the freedom of art is in its liberation of the artist from received form. A further statement of this truth might be that it frees one to move through subjectivity—and beyond it. "I believe it is impossible," Hayden Carruth says, "to write a poem, a real poem, that is not an expression of subjectivity moving through and beyond itself." Certainly free verse, at its best moments, has for me the feeling almost of an ur-language, original and personal and accurate, language straining toward the ultimate/essential individual, yet nonetheless free of the ac- cidence of place, time, person. And those who do not hear the music of such language, the beauty of it, are, I believe, either tone deaf or not listening.

This language is, we feel, authentic language. But what au- thenticates language? Is it some external standard it can be placed over against, like checking the diameter of a strand of wire? Or is it something inside, something that makes you know the words are touching feeling, words that are not clothes but bodies. Or maybe I should say, not androids but real, navel-marked bodies, bearing a density and range of feel- ing about them that declares this is what it means to be human. Authentic language rises, Robert Bly says somewhere, from ev- ery depth. And I believe it. Authentic language speaks from inside. And the authenticity of the whole gesture (the essential poem) bears itself into you the reader, so that its body and your body become, for a time, one. Stanley Plumly's "Rainbow" is an instance:

> Taking its time
> through each of the seven vertebrae of light
> the sun comes down. It is nineteen forty-nine.
> You stand in the doorway drying your hands.
> It is still summer, still raining.
> The evening is everywhere gold: windows, grass,
> the sun side of the trees. As if to speak
> to someone you look back into the dark
> of the house, call my name, go in. I know
> I am dreaming again. Still, it is raining
> and the sun shining . . . You come back out

into the doorway, shading your eyes. It looks
as if the whole sky is going down on one wing.
By now I have my hands above my eyes, listening.

The true importance of Carruth's point about the real poem
moving through subjectivity arises from the fact that each person is humanity. That is a profound fact for a poem to touch,
to reveal to us. "You look back into the dark / of the house, call
my name, go in." A mythic knowledge. The abidingly personal.

Jung said that the American Indian has constituted the single
most powerful force in the formation of the American unconscious, that even the skyline of a city like Chicago reestablishes
the layout outline of an Indian pueblo. Likewise, I believe the
poetic form of our time (which we have called free verse)
bodies forth the life we live, conscious and unconscious. And
for American poets, that's a life this land speaks (and sings)
through. And what is it we're hearing there? What the music?
I suggest it is the music we hum while we sleep. Songs that
know us by name. What we hear when we press our ear close to
the earth we are, the places everyone we love lives to death in.

Perhaps the poetry, this body of poetry, is our ongoing attempt to find the holophrase that would name it, the one that
keeps trying to rise up into our mouth from trees, from hills,
from refrigerators, from vapor trails horses never look up to.
In James Wright it is Ohio and West Virginia, a countryside
drowsing and dreaming, spilling west across Minnesota, North
Dakota, Montana, the earth turning our feet to mud, our
lives floating face-down in the Ohio, in the Mississippi. Mid-
western ditches half-filled with snow, cornfields, barns, hay-
mows, rural mailboxes, deserted streets of small towns. The
nonurban American earth—rocks, streams, mountains, trees,
sky. These are the places you find it. Or else in the towns, frequently with names from England, from Europe: New London, Rome, Paris, Athens, Oxford, New York, Gloucester. But
now each town carries a larger name, one with its own people

in it: their tongues, their lives, their deaths. These are the names we've found/had to find a language for. A form for.

I believe I have been speaking throughout here of prosody. We all know the wonder of Whitman's free verse, seemingly as sudden in its arrival as the discovery of gravity. Or perhaps relativity. We recognize in it the prosody of the democratic ideal, of physical exuberance, of optimism, of geographic largeness. The prosody of American names, of scope, of plenitude. The prosody of rivers and forests. Of the hat on indoors. His prosody embraces all this. Is all this. And this is not merely a larger sense of prosody; it is, I believe, a truer one. Similarly, by "form" we must surely be prepared to accommodate notions of inner form (structures of imagery and feeling, of symbols; or, to borrow from Hayden Carruth, "scarcely revealed nodes of imaginative energy") and outer form (syntax, diction, patterns of sound and imagery, sentence and phrasal rhythms, etc.). A new form is a new idea, we quote the imagists. Form *is* the poem, we add. And know it is true. "I and this mystery," Whitman says, "here we stand."

In the best contemporary poetry—almost all of it in free verse—the prosody, for me, carries an equally extensive, and significant, freight. For example, as a prosody of angst, of imperfection, of mortality. M. L. Rosenthal has said that a powerful stroke of memory is necessary to the creation of poetry. He is of course thinking of memory as Proust described it: "The smell and taste of things remain poised a long time, like souls, ready to remind us, waiting and hoping for their moment, amid the ruins of all the rest; and bear unfalteringly, in the tiny and almost impalpable drop of their essence, the vast structure of recollection." And it is surely true. But additionally, memory carries unmistakable within it the seeds of dread, of uncertainty. We hear it in, for example, the poems of the Eskimos of Canada and Greenland (a strictly oral culture), which bear to us again and again the fear that they would forget their song (poem) and the sense that the poem was an important, a fundamental, extension of self. But fragile, vulnerable:

> Life was wonderful
> when you danced in the feasting house;
> but did this make me any happier?
> No, I always worried
> I'd forget my song.

Inherent in this anxiety is the knowledge that poems—one's words, one's spirit—can be forgotten. Perhaps the Eskimo poet Piuvkaq speaks for us too:

> It's wonderful
> to make up songs:
> but all too often many of them fail.
> It's wonderful
> to have your wishes granted:
> but all too often
> they slip by.
> It's wonderful
> to hunt reindeer:
> but all too seldom
> you succeed
> standing like a bright fire
> on the plain.

Such poetry finds human ontology in memory. For it is memory that, knowing the past, posits the future. Or perhaps it is enough to say that it posits the past. For that already brings nonbeing into the present. Here memory is, we might say, a moment of mortality. There is about it a sense of inevitable loss, of disappearance, of grief. And we hear it in our poems. As Galway Kinnell's *The Book of Nightmares* has it: "being forever / in the pretrembling of a house that falls." Indeed *The Book of Nightmares* seems to me almost a paradigm for the "formal" meaning of our free verse. What this book finds out, what

it knows, is that "the wages / of dying is love." "Yes," the poem
"Under the Maud Moon" says:

> You cling because
> I, like you, only sooner
> than you, will go down
> the path of vanished alphabets.

The Book of Nightmares seems to me paradigmatic because it is a
poetry of loss, of mortality, of imperfection.

> We who live out our plain lives, who put
> our hand into the hand of whatever we love
> as it vanishes,
> as we vanish,
> and stumble toward what will be, simply by arriving,
> a kind of fate . . .

Kinnell might almost as well have said a kind of life. Or a kind
of poem. This song, this poem, even in the moment of vanishing ("lighting ourselves up so completely we are vanishing"), is.
We remember D. H. Lawrence's distinction between form that
defends and form which exposes. The latter kind allows something to be present. As in James Wright's "To Flood Stage
Again":

> In Fargo, North Dakota, a man
> Warned me the river might rise
> To flood stage again.
> On the bridge, a girl hurries past me, alone,
> Unhappy face.
> Will she pause in wet grass somewhere?
> Behind my eyes she stands tiptoe, yearning
>   for confused sparrows
> To fetch a bit of string and dried wheatbeard
> To line her outstretched hand.
> I open my eyes and gaze down
> At the dark water.

Suddenly present in the poem is desperation, despair. We do not view the anguish through a window in an umbrella. Here, all at once, it is. It makes our eyes flare like a mare's.

Any single instant of a human being's experience is, we know, infinitely fuller than any amount of detailed explanation, explication, or analysis can possibly exhaust—much less recreate. Yet this is precisely what we ask our best poems to do: to recreate that content. And of course the best of them do, astoundingly, just that. And when they do, that moment—in its aesthetic, literary, verbal, genuinely human recapture—is manifest in "adequate" form. For the poet—the person making the gesture of the spirit that is poetry—writing a poem is always a search for adequate form, a search for what will embody that dense experience/perception/urge/ultimatum that the throat and tongue are attempting to say. What I am referring to with the phrase "adequate form" is nothing less than the actual, finite presence in the poem of the totality of content that a moment of human experience contains. In Coleridgean terms, that experience is sustained by "the eternal act of creation in the Infinite I Am." Its palpable presence in the poem then is, in these terms, "the repetition in the finite mind."

Philip Levine has said of Kinnell's poetry that he is "asking his language to transfigure our experience." Certainly the poems of *The Book of Nightmares*—in their grief, their compassion, their love, their cry of pain, of not-knowing—are a search. For words. For adequate form. For a body to hold this spirit. All of *The Book of Nightmares* can be seen as a quest (remembering the root kinship with question, with uncertainty). Poem after poem arcs through an articulation of questions, or a search for certainty or comfort. But equally—perhaps more than equally—they declare our physical life on earth: moonlaved, starchilled. And the poems declare love for it. And through it. Arresting the fall even in the act of falling.

These poems, like us, live only in time. And they exist in the always tensional relationship between, on the one hand, knowledge that we are "two mismatched halfnesses lying side by side

in the darkness" and, on the other, the conviction that wholeness, oneness, is possible:

> that purest,
> most tragic concumbence, strangers
> clasped into one, a moment, of their moment on earth.

Strangely, however, the poems do not deny perfection; they
assert it: it is everywhere discovered by the language, the reach,
the quest of the poem. But primarily it is known in our fleshly
failure to achieve it. Or hold it. Or maintain it.

> You feel all your bones
> break
> over the holy waters you will never drink.
>
> .   .   .   .
>
> All bodies, one body, one light
> made of everyone's darkness together . . .
>
> .   .   .   .
>
> We shall not all sleep, but we shall be changed . . .
>
> .   .   .   .
>
> As the creation
> touches him a last time all over his body . . .
>
> .   .   .   .
>
> . . . in the graveyard
> the lamps start lighting up, one for each of us,
> in all the windows
> of stone.

Thus in one sense the form of these poems is the *in*-forming
of grief. Also the informing of mortal imperfection, the per-
fectly human imperfection that brings forth our song.

> This poem,
> if we shall call it that,
> or concert of one
> divided among himself,
> this earthward gesture
> of the sky-diver, the worms

> on his back still spinning forth
> and already gnawing away
> the silks of his loves, who could have saved him,
> this free floating of one
> opening his arms into the attitude
> of flight, as he obeys the necessity and falls . . .

Language, movement, images—all of this is the transfiguring fall. It embodies the full knowledge—emotional, intellectual, sensory—which the poem gains in its mortal quest.

> And do the dead wings creak open as we
> soar across the wings of the bear?

The poetry is a purely human marrying of opposites, its language and its gestures the dark sparkles of eternity forever lost. However one might scan any of these (or other) lines, whatever rhythmic nuances we might be able to note in them, whatever rhetorical patterns identify—this seems to me inescapable: the mystery and confusion, the paradox and dark splendor of our existence are everywhere affirmed. Especially is this so in the formal aspects: the absence of transcendental certainty, the impossibility of forms that know more than we are, forms that would assert healing we cannot know, that would declare perfections our own bodies cannot live in.

I think we have here been looking at the prosody of poems that, like our lives, are time-bound, time-defined. Poems that call out to us across the darkness of the valley of not-knowing. I, for one, always answer: "yes? yes?"

During the decades of our work, in our search for adequate form, we have taken our own lives as pole star. And if we would be serious about form, if we would be true to it, we must talk about it so. We cannot measure it as we would the diameter of wire, nor judge it by standards that speak of experiences not our own. And we must not be put off by foolish quarrels and false definitions of the problem. Gabriel Marcel has warned us of the desire of most people to reduce a mystery to a problem.

For problems are capable of solution. Mysteries are not. "The more closely scientists look at life and its evolution," says Jonathan Schell in *The Fate of the Earth*, "the less they find it possible to draw a sharp distinction between 'life,' on the one hand, and an inanimate 'environment' in which it exists, on the other. Rather, 'the environment' of the present day appears to be a house of unimaginable intricacy which life has to a very great extent built and furnished for its own use."

Substitute "form" for "environment" and "poetry" for "life" and you have, I think, the poetry of our time. It's enough to shame silliness out of you.

Some Notes toward Sincerity

The term "sincerity" has often been used to try to point to something that is essential to writing we can trust, writing we can believe in. What he required of a writer, Thoreau said, "first or last, [is] a simple and sincere account of his own life . . . some such account as he would send to his kindred from a distant land." "In sincerity," Louis Zukovsky wrote, "writing occurs which is the *detail* of seeing, of thinking with things as they exist." *Detail*, of course, is the crucial word here. And consider Wallace Stevens's statement, that the poet writes what he hears and sees, for then he "feels its presence."

Presence. That is what we are after: the sense of fullness, the sense of Being itself, its living presence. And what is required of the poet is a sense of responsibility to *the world as we experience it*. What the poet "hears" and "sees"—the detail of seeing—is what carries us back and down into the experience, the world *as experienced*. What is required, in other words, is attention—sincere attention, i.e., responsibility—to the detail of seeing, the detail of experiencing, in order that *inherent*

meaning might emerge—what Merleau-Ponty calls the deci-
sive moment of perception: "the upsurge of a true and accurate world."

*

*Poetry is that intercommunication between the inner being of things
and the inner being of the human self.*

— Jacques Maritain

*

Even in my simplest pieces, even in the shortest poems, this is
what I aim for. I do not want to "relate" something or "narrate"
something, but to make something present. The poem does
not wish to say what I believe or what I understand, but to
present what is. Being is its object and desire, being its goal.

Of course the mind *participates* in being, is itself a part of its
mysterious and constant surge into form into substance into
awareness into words.

In this participation the poem lives. In sincerity participation is
experienced.

*

This aesthetic attitude, this "spiritual" disposition of one toward one's art, this total belief in it as both result *and process*, is
not, I know all too well, easily arrived at. It requires a certain
humility, as well as a clarity (or purity) of perception/under-
standing. It requires not only an ability to invoke the formal
powers of the art but, equally important, a trust in those powers, a *belief* in them, an almost prayerful invocation of them as
one attempts to recall and enact being. In this attitude—and
this use—the formal qualities of poetry are never used for effect, never "devices" employed as strategies of communication.

"Speech and understanding," says Merleau-Ponty, "are moments in the unified system of self-other." And "Communica-

tion," Barbara Herrnstein Smith reminds us, "is not the motive of thinking."

Or as Michael Heller puts it: A "poem is not an attempt to reach others but is the very form of our interconnectedness."

✳

Poetry is the act of preserving the world from indifference, from simple otherness. It is an act of witnessing, a revelation of *human* instance.

> *It is when one is in extreme thirst,*
> *ill with thirst; then one no longer thinks of the act*
> *of drinking in relation to oneself, or even the act of drinking*
>
> *in a general way. One merely thinks of water,*
> *actual water itself, but the image of water is like a cry*
> *from our whole being.*
>
> – Simone Weil

✳

Does such an approach somehow limit the range of one's engagement in a poem? I don't think so. But it does, no doubt, alter one's relationship to the matter, reduce, perhaps, the will's role in the work. For myself, I want to make everything I know available to a poem. But so far as I can see, this desire has very little to do with any discursive *setting forth* of either information or ideas. Indeed I believe that this desire has in fact been most nearly realized in some of my "smallest" poems, poems that essay very little of either exposition or narrative, poems of, in fact, relatively small word count.

"I still have trouble with verbs," says George Oppen. "It's not exactly trouble: I just didn't want to put it too pretentiously. I'm really concerned with the substantive, with the subject of the sentence, with what we are talking about, and not rushing over the subject-matter to make a comment about it. . . . The important thing is that if we are talking about the nature of reality, then we are not really talking about our comment about it; we are talking about the apprehension of some *thing*, whether it is or not, whether one can make a thing of it or not."

*

And what are some of the *formal* implications of this stretch for sincerity? In other words, what is the relationship between the poet (the person) and the form?

One way to engage this question is to consider some of the built-in liabilities, or dangers, in what we might call "received" forms, forms that inescapably bring with themselves an established and definite range of both content and association, the kind of dowry that Donald Barthelme is thinking of when he says that a writer's first responsibility is "the silencing of an existing rhetoric."

Consider first some of the time-honored ways of viewing the formal qualities of poetry in the English tradition, what is commonly referred to as poetry in traditional forms:

That these forms are themselves an institutionalized source
  of wisdom and insight.
That they represent some peculiarly accurate "discoveries"
  about language and mind and matter.
That these forms are *inherent* in human experience.
That (particularly as respects language, rhyme, meter, etc.)
  they are *natural* to English; even, sometimes, that the
  rhythms they describe are the *only* English rhythms.
That these forms bring *order* to the material of our
  experience (the implication being that such material is,
  without these forms, lacking order).

Consider next some of the possible sources of tension between received, or "traditional," forms and twentieth-century thought/experience:

These forms seem to posit certainty, where uncertainty is
  the content of our existential condition.

They substitute fixity for change, result for process.
They declare absolutes in a universe of relativity.

And in human, individual experience, consider the tension between patterns that express perfection (e.g., closure, rhyme,
fixed meters, etc.) and an experience that knows, or embodies,
imperfection. (In this regard, notice how irony in modernism
was already a manifestation of this tension, a deliberate under-
cutting of the forms of expression themselves. This tension is
especially present in the work of such late modernists as Wilbur
and Lowell and Berryman. In irony the destruction of those
things being undercut is already, incipiently at least, present,
already accomplished. They have ceased to be trusted.)

These tensions may be, in our time, inevitable. Certainly they
are profound in their effect on the sincere efforts artists will
make as they attempt to engage the life we are living. As, indeed, are the following ones:

> The tension between a view of poetry as versified
> "communication" and a view of poetry as discovery/
> incarnation.

> The tension between the recognition by modern physics
> that chance plays a role inside the atom, and forms that
> do not acknowledge chance, that cannot admit its
> presence. Here, even irony won't work for long. As we
> know, art in the twentieth century has found itself
> struggling steadily to find ways of acknowledging the
> presence of chance, or random events, in its work.

> And consider the further increase of this tension that has
> been caused by the thinking in physics that calls into
> question the reality of the heretofore "real" world, i.e.,
> thinking that has robbed the phenomenal, the appearing
> world, of its solid, unquestioned *external* existence, in
> favor of the world of subatomic physics. And we
> recognize some of the important philosophical

implications of these thoughts: for instance, that there is clearly no room here for a simply "objective" world, for it must be seen to be itself deeply involved with the subjective: In short, the recognition that the world of "appearances"—that is, the *phenomena*—is a world in which the perceiver is a *primary* element. (Is this also, perhaps, a promising context in which to consider the growth of the dominant *I* in contemporary poetry?)

Of course there are a host of other possible tensions one could cite, including those that arise from a recognition of the irrational, the discontinuous, the irreconcilable in our lives, and the need to accommodate these thoughts, these experiences. But what is perhaps most important for us to see are some of the "dangers" these tensions help us to recognize, the dangers that cause us to feel the need to "silence an existing rhetoric."

These dangers stem primarily, it seems to me, from the power of the formal expressions of such rhetoric to reduce, to avoid, to fail to discover. They tend, we have felt, to distract us from more fundamental matters, the poem as discovery, for instance. If, as Frost said, "no surprise in the writer, no surprise in the reader," where, we ask, and how, is surprise likeliest to occur? Also what kind of surprise? As Galway Kinnell has said, the problems traditional forms ask the poet to solve are of a different sort from those of what we might call open forms, more mechanical than psychic. And therein lies perhaps the greatest danger. For if these forms distract us from—or, worse, cause us to avoid—discovery and insight, then they have a liability to lead us to untruths—to self-deception even, as well as to complacency and conventionality of thought and feeling; to lead us, as Marvin Bell has put it, "to tell elegant lies."

Surely one of the elements that has led to the growth in importance of the image in American poetry in the second half of the century is this recognition, this awareness: awareness of the image's role as instrument of discovery, as touchstone of truth, as way into self; all of which comes from a felt need to get something clean, something pure, something believable, but also from the conviction that the image is not an *illustration* of something, of some postulated meaning, but rather that it is the *very source and form* of an idea. It comes from an inescapable realization that "meaning" is not limited to, or even identical with, one's "intention."

There are also the dangers that come from a reduction of *formal* possibilities: the danger that a willful adherence to certain received forms may lead also to an acquiescence in the claims of their rhetorical hangers-on, with their soiled baggage, together with those of a large troop of camp followers whispering their comforting sentiments and perceptions, their deceptions and insincerities. This danger is of course closely linked to the one that comes from the obscuring, by one music, of a truer one, possibly a more personal one. For we are here speaking of the poet, not as dictator, but as citizen; we are speaking of the mind as participatory, not as explanatory or "formgiving." The poet's need is to hear a "music" he or she can trust, a music that is in truth a source, not an expression. A music that both tests and *reveals* sincerity.

For Americans, of course, the need—and the long struggle— has been to find *our* language, with its rhythms and places: the names, the topography, the farms and cities; the smells, the sights, the tastes of the continent. The need has been, and must continue to be, to *discover* America. To find it again and again perhaps. In ourselves. In our art.

And will not this, of necessity, bring surprise—the surprise of true encounter, of insight and discovery?

I believe none of what I have said here implies abandonment. Rather, it implies enlargement—of both possibility and awareness. Awareness, for example, of the importance of the formal features of the poem's appearance on the page, its lines and its stanzas, what they look like, how they move, how they

determine themselves and each other. How they reveal un-
foreseen symmetries and connections, unlooked-for harmonies and unions. For poetry is not a game, with or without a
net; is not a calculated playing for effect. Our best poets today
seem to have found themselves encountering poetry as both
instrument and occasion of search, of uncompromising exploration: as journey into the interior of the troubled, troubling,
exhilarating, awesome being we are part of. A journey that is
at every step a test of their sincerity. The best poetry, of course,
always knew this, always did this. For this is at the heart of the
adventure that poetry is.

Needless to say, there are still poetry-as-parlor game writers.
But their work seems to us to have little to do with the sincere
search, the risks into being, to which the best work keeps re-
turning. And in thinking of them we may recall a passage from
Thoreau's journal: "The way in which men cling to old institu-
tions after the life has departed out of them, and out of themselves, reminds me of those monkeys which cling by their
tails,—aye, whose tails contract about the limbs, even the dead
limbs, of the forest, and they hang suspended beyond the
hunter's reach long after they are dead. It is of no use to argue
with such men. They have not an apprehensive intellect, but
merely, as it were, a prehensile tail. . . . The tail itself contracts
around the dead limb even after they themselves are dead, and
not till sensible corruption takes place do they fall."

✳

In sincerity one's poems will always dwell in the valley above
which, in all seasons, these questions tower:

How do we know this?
Where does the knowledge come from?
*What source are we trying to tap, as we search for words, images,
    rhythms, patterns?*
What are we trying to be responsible to?

And asleep or waking, their feet will be laved by the dark waters of uncertainty. As Jung says, "The psyche cannot leap beyond itself. It cannot set up any absolute truths, for its own polarity determines the relativity of its statements." Indeed, "the not-knowing," Donald Barthelme reminds us, "is crucial to art, is what permits art to be made."

And so the questions swarm back:

> *Where is the "meaning" going to be found?*
> *Where shall we look for it?*
> *How do we begin the search? How continue it?*
> *If poetry is knowing more than we are conscious of, how do we gain*
>   *access to that knowledge?*

*

The poems' form, of course, is their answer—the bodies they stand forth in, light falling on their bright hair, their shoulders: their sensual curves into dark.

How is conviction, how is sincerity, shown in a poem except as (or in) form—form as the honest desire to evoke and embody, the poem as *enactment* of becoming:

>   to hold the world a moment
>   forever
>
>   in its constant
>   fall
>
>   from light

*

The pure prosaic can apprehend nothing but results. It knows naught of the thing coming into being, only of the thing become. It cannot realize shapes. It sees nature—and would like to see art—as a series of mechanical arrangements of facts. And facts are facta, things done and past.

– Owen Barfield

*

To see: To hear: To recognize. This is the requirement, the need, that the sincere writer faces. This is the need that underlies the attempts "to face in the right direction," in order that one might be in a position possibly to glimpse, though perhaps only fleetingly, something essential. Where to look, also to listen: For being. For presence.

The poet must assume an attitude that will allow him or her to make this contact, this discovery, this linkage between the spoken and the unspoken. World as meaning. The poem phenomenally appearing. The page as aspect of "the detail of seeing": the lines that emerge there, their certain movements on the ground of our seeing, the voices they bear into the world we share with them, the awarenesses we are together.

There is where our sincerity will be proved—that is, both tested and revealed.

There is where we will "see" the moments of perception that the poem both participates in and embodies.

There is where connections will be discovered, harmonies found.

There is where words may arc suddenly into sight across the white silence of space, where language may show itself forth as physical matter—body and spirit as one, language as the existent thing itself: the metaphor of being, emerging and acting itself out before us.

Horizontal

"Nature," Cézanne declared, "must be treated in terms of the cylinder, the cone, and the sphere," an attitude still present to a certain extent even in Cubism's dislocational explorations of the world's body. When, however, one comes to the work of the abstract expressionists, what seems at once both striking and profoundly significant is the almost complete absence of such thinking, such seeing.

What we do hear, somewhere in the background of this radical "new" art, are such thoughts as this one articulated by Werner Haftmann: "The modern experience of form . . . [is] the experience of a concrete reality, which belongs to the human mind alone, and in which the mind represents itself." Or this one by Wassily Kandinsky: "On the question of form, it makes no difference whether the artist uses real or abstract forms."

What we become aware of, in short, is the emergence of a notion that came to stand at the very center of much of the twentieth century's thinking about art: namely, that once the artist is freed from delineating a thing, whatever he or she paints "functions as a thing in itself."

Today we are keenly aware of the "theoretical" distance that separates such thinking, such seeing, from that of a generation or so earlier. And we recognize what an immense distance that is.

But do we truly understand some of the farther-reaching implications of this distance, this separation?

I wonder.

Well might we ask ourselves, for instance, "What ever happened to the 'familiar' world in this continued movement away from a concern with art as 'representation' to a concern with art as 'being' or art as 'enactment'?" Wistfully might we wonder, "Where did it go, then, that lovely world of forms?"

For a partial answer one might consider the paintings of Mark Rothko.

An aspect of the paintings of Rothko's mature phase which both fascinates and challenges as we try to understand their power is the way they are fundamentally focused on the horizontal. In this focus Rothko seems somehow to have perceived (and "perceived" is surely the word) a primary connection between ourselves and the appearing world of "nature"; seems somehow to have actually seen an essential connection. Here, in this experiential fact of seeing and being, Rothko found something so fundamental, something so humanly elemental, that it "abstracts" both the physical and experiential worlds to their purest existence: both the purely physical and the purely spiritual. They exist as one in the horizontal—the horizontal lines the paintings declare to us, the horizontal lines we always find the world in, and as.

What is reflected in this focus, I believe, is the important recognition that "horizon" is a primary, an elemental, focus of our seeing; that it is expression of our very rootedness on the earth: our sense of physical belonging, our knowledge of home. Wherever we look, it is ground. Even when we sleep, horizon holds us and maintains us, defends our bodies and souls from the angst of freefall. Waking or sleeping, we see the solid reassurance of the horizontal. Before us, around us, the planet spreads its phenomenal mass, spreads out and focuses our seeing. We stand upon the seen firmament stretching always away from us horizontally, and so, like those strange shadows of ourselves the animals, we commit ourselves trustingly to its promise. Daily we lie down into the mystery of sleep, the great mother beneath us, around us, and know: everything that rises up from the plane that sustains us, everything that strives up vertically beside us, is fixed to that firm ground of perception.

These horizontal lines by their very nature—by our very nature—participate in our knowledge of the earth: its very existence, our very existence. Rothko's mature paintings know this, offer this perception. In his paintings our deep knowledge of the horizontal is evoked by the presence of rectangular blocks of color, colors which echo the natural world—greens, browns, grays, blacks, yellows. And of course the colors are vital, crucial. But what one wants to stress is that these blocks of color do not somehow "represent" the natural world—that world of vegetation and minerals and water and animals. Nor would it be enough—or even, I believe, quite accurate—to say that any of these paintings "suggest" the natural world. What happens here and what is present here is something more important than that, something more fundamental than that. The "seeing" of these paintings participates completely in that ground knowledge of the horizontal which I have been discussing. They invoke its absolute presence; they evoke our existence in it. The shapes and colors which they present are not just primary, they are essential. They are essence—of our knowledge of ourselves on earth. In this knowledge, horizon dominates; it is everywhere. And because of it, there is, in the paintings, space.

And there is also mass. Above the mass of the earth's enclosed body, there is openness. It is above us: sleeping or waking we know it is there.

And below it there is body.

This is the context in which all verticality exists in the paintings; it implicates our knowing—both conscious and unconscious—at the most primary level. It is perception as existence—the pure, abstracted essence made physically present. In these blocks of color, in their tensions and equilibrium, mass is enabled at once to float and to remain fixed. And we, looking upon them, feel again the deep thrill of being.

As for Rothko himself, a painting he did in the last year of his life (*Untitled, Black and Gray*, 1970) makes perhaps the most daring (the ultimate?) declaration: *there is only horizon, only the horizontal*, the statement completely undefended by any hints of other shapes or colors or mass. There is only the line—our mortal existence on earth, its essential participation in gravity. Below the line, there is only an expanse of unachieved gray; above it, only the huge, unbroken blackness. Totally absent from this vision: all suggestion of sky, all vitality of color, all upthrust of life-forms, all phenomenal presence.

This perception—or discovery—of the primacy of the horizontal appears to have been one shared to some extent by other modernist painters, especially in the middle decades of this century. Hans Hoffman, Philip Guston, Adolph Gottlieb, for instance—all show this awareness, this recognition of the power these spatial presences and tensions have to touch our deepest knowledge of the physical world. In perception, the phenomenal world has somehow been abstracted to its essential "physicality"—which is also, simultaneously, its essential spirituality. For what we see here—what we experience here—is the inseparability of the world's body and our involved awareness of it.

In Adolph Gottlieb's painting *Bias Pull*, for instance, the painting is, like Rothko's paintings, dominated by horizontals of mass and shape (blocks), with their invocation of solidity and weight. But here there is the added presence of two major bars of black on a bias to the horizontals, so located that they exert a constant diagonal tug upward—on us where we stand, on the earth where we stand. The level that perception reaches to here is like that of our knowledge of our own heartbeat. It is at the level of participation: we do not look at, we look into. We become. We, and the world that sustains us, exist at that moment in the living presence of nature, life as us and life in us, the presence of a few lesser bias-pulls in the lower right one-third of the painting implicating us still further in the material world of nascent forms. Our bodies know it: they feel it in their long miles of blood and sinew and nerves, in the minute constellations of corpuscles, molecules, atoms.

Heinz Pagels tells us of experiments showing that when one presents simultaneously to a viewer, as in a stereopticon, two images which separately consist entirely of purely random spots but taken together have some sort of correlation, the eye/mind will, after only a few moments of looking, perceive the pattern that is in the correlation, so that the pattern will stand forth from the background of chaos as if in three dimensions. Further, if months later the same images are shown again to the viewer, the mind will instantly see again that pattern, that order, that physical presence of form.

In this experiment physicists and philosophers have recognized, among other important implications, another clear indication of the mind's innate sensitivity to form, its dedication to form. Form, shape, pattern—these aspects of the phenomenal appearance of the world are also aspects of the mind itself. These aspects, when joined with the potentiality of external stimuli, stand forth as the phenomena we know as world, its physical presence. Likewise, three-quarters of a century of steady pursuit of the implications of "quantum reality" has brought contemporary science to a recognition of the "truth" of the insight arrived at by Max Born and Werner Heisenberg as early as 1927: At the atomic level, the "objective" world does not exist except when and as it is observed. The idea of an objective world that is always and independently present, whether or not anyone is there to see it, has been shattered by the implications of quantum thinking. "Our very physics shouts it at us," Owen Barfield says: "Nature herself is the representation of man."

Such a recognition is at the heart of the thinking of the phenomenologists. And this thinking is underscored by the undeniable fact that our best efforts to probe into the very heart of matter have steadily shown that, at some level, the "objectivity" of matter simply disappears, to be replaced by a view of reality that finds it impossible to locate its atomic components in space (as objects) and at the same time remain true to the certain evidence of its existence as a sequence of pure probability.

In the subatomic "world" that quantum physics explores, particle (whose position one can precisely determine) and wave (the measure of its momentum) must be seen as complementary concepts—meaning they are mutually exclusive. "Physicists," Pagels writes, in *The Cosmic Code*, "speak of the particle representation or the wave representation. Bohr's principle of complementarity asserts that there exist complementary properties of the same object of knowledge, one of which if known will exclude knowledge of the other. We may therefore describe an object like an electron in ways which are mutually exclusive—as a wave or a particle—without logical contradiction provided we also realize that the experimental arrangements that determine these descriptions are similarly mutually exclusive. Which experiment—and hence which description—one chooses is purely a matter of human choice." This view, known as the Copenhagen interpretation, and which accommodates both the uncertainty principle of Heisenberg and the indeterminacy principle of Born, makes it possible for us to realize that such distinctions as location and movement are, at some level, arbitrary; that they are, in fact, at some level impossible to make. And this interpretation—this stabilizing understanding for quantum physics—reminds us how difficult it is to find a language with which to "think" about this new knowledge concerning the material world—the world we live in. With Niels Bohr we are led to question the adequacy of our grammar to speak of this knowledge, its adequacy to describe the reality there indicated. This is, of course, as Bohr recognized, a language problem; for the grammar of our language both guides and limits our thinking, empowers and restricts it. It is also obviously a cultural problem; for the attitudes and beliefs and expectations we have about the world—about "reality"—are deeply embedded in the language we use to speak of it—to question it, to describe it, to declare it; even, as in poetry, to embody it.

The implications of these ideas are, needless to say, far-reaching. They are also, it should be unnecessary to add, unavoidable. Paramount among them, as physicists know, is the fact that the subatomic level of reality is a statistical one, a level of probabilities, a level that does not answer to the demands of a grammar based on the world of sensory data. It is a reality, in other words, that does not have "objective" meaning, as in the world of classical physics. Thus one must say with the physicist John Wheeler, "No phenomenon is a phenomenon until it is an observed phenomenon." For the overwhelming evidence is that though matter does surely exist, it does not exist as "object" except as it involves the observer. To the extent that it "appears" as phenomena, to that same extent we, as perceivers, are implicated.

In short, the world of nature is truly our world—even as we are its. The appearing features of the physical world—its shapes, its colors, its textures, its smells—these are "patterns" specific to us, patterns innate in us, patterns we stand forth as, bodying forth out of the atomic potentiality of the world the vision we equally participate in. This world of forms is our very selves. The trees, the rocks, the water, light, the haunting curve of wing or arm against a field of blue: all this is our being on earth, our emergence in time as instant of perception—the quantum world of probability fixing itself, with us, in time; its wave of indeterminacy entering, irreversibly, the objective existence individual lives are measured by, the existence they begin, and end, as.

Form is what we perceive. Form is what we desire. Form is our own "nature," longing to be achieved, longing to be seen, longing to be felt. Longing to be whole. It is what our psychical/ physical selves participate in at their most primary level, their deepest level. As form, the world is perceived. And as form we perceive it. Recognize it. Know its integral presence in ourselves. Its presence as ourselves. Mind and body

as one. Here, we realize, the world appears by its very nature as metaphor: the appearing phenomena always signaling the structure of correspondence that underlies them, the way in which being is always, at some level, also meaning.

The physical appearance of the phenomenal world always represents the ordering structure that gives it form. One could say, therefore, that it represents, or looks beyond itself toward, the structures of order and meaning that give it being—i.e., the spirit both of mind and of appearing nature.

This, it seems to me, is something like what the Romantics were thinking of when they spoke of "natural metaphor," or when Coleridge was defining the imagination. Clearly Coleridge recognized that whatever quality gave the mind the power to sustain in perception the order and form of the natural world must be inherently the same as the one that sustains this order and form in Nature. "The primary imagination I hold to be the living power and prime agent of all human perception, and as a repetition in the finite mind of the eternal act of creation in the Infinite I am."

In other words, the world of phenomena is by nature a metaphoric one. The individual phenomenon both is and means, stands complete and at the same time refers. And this, I would suggest, is the quality art strives to be at one with. Art wishes to experience again the phenomenal world, the actual world of phenomena, the world of mass and color and shape and texture, the world of the senses; it wishes to experience it so fully, wishes to make it, somehow, so present, that it will carry within itself all the powerful presence of the physical world, and at the same time reveal the great presence of the spiritus mundi, which we both suffer and act as. Throughout the ages art has, it seems to me, expressed this need, this desire, this possibility.

But the subatomic world—the quantum world—does exist. And for most of this century, this aspect of reality has formed a central tenet of scientific and philosophic thought. It is a fundamental part of our belief system about reality. Its basic principles have become, to some degree, a part of the "world view" of all educated persons. Who does not know, for example, that "the very act of observation changes what is observed"?—even though he or she may never have really "thought" about the implications of that statement. In short, the thinking of quantum physics has become a part of our structure of belief about the physical world. It has become part of the structure of our thought and of our expectations. To some extent, I would say, it has become an aspect of our "experience"—perhaps even of our primary experience—of the world.

Increasingly through much of the last century or so the various arts appear to have felt the need to "see" at an even more primary level, have attempted, in various ways, to bring nearer to the level of consciousness what happens—or used to happen—at the level of the unconscious. In some instances, even the very event of perception has been looked at, or into.

This steady movement in art has expressed not a reduction but a re-emphasis of the importance of the formal qualities of a work. It has been a constant demonstration to us that, as Susan Sontag has reminded us, we must not take the sensory element of art for granted. It has been a way of reaffirming the central fact of the sensory in art—in poetry no less than in painting. It has been a way artists have found to make themselves—ourselves—see more, touch more, hear more. More than that, however, it has been an attempt to move the aesthetic response ever closer to its source in the mind itself and, thereby, to the phenomenal world, which we experience the profound mystery of being in. And in this respect it has increasingly emphasized the epistemological function of form—that is, its essential involvement in what and how we know.

All this is fairly obvious, of course. What is perhaps less obvious is the extent to which this more or less steady drive away from representation of an "objective" world not only paralleled the disappearance of that world from the thought of scientists and philosophers but also reflected an increasing "consciousness" of the preconscious activity of the mind, almost as if the borderline between the two had moved somehow, with the result that some of what before had occurred strictly at the preconscious level had come to seem something one could almost see happening, almost be conscious of. Owen Barfield seemed to be looking toward some such alteration when he said, writing of the impressionist painters, "They really painted nature in the light of the eye, as no other painters had done before them. They were striving to realize in consciousness the normally unconscious activity of 'figuration' itself. They did not imitate; they expressed 'themselves'—inasmuch as they painted nature as the representation of man." (The term "figuration" here refers to the organizing function of the perceiving mind in the act of perception, the act of organizing, at a preconscious level, the external world's potential into the phenomena that we are actually conscious of.)

"As far as our conscious experience is concerned," Barfield says, "the perceptual world comes over its horizon already organized. But who has done the organizing? What are you going to call this preconscious organizing of perceptual experience, which gives us the world as we actually and consciously experience it? Coleridge called it 'primary imagination.'"

Perhaps the indeterminacy/uncertainty in quantum mechanics implies, as some have suggested, that the quanta are somehow responding to the unconscious. But more clearly, and more certainly, it implies that prior to entering the phenomenal world, the subatomic structure of the physical world exists as potentials.

And what about art? Can we experience, in our language or in our art, that moment of "realization," that moment when potential becomes actual, the moment when the subatomic structure of the world enters existence, the "natural" world accomplished in particular instants of time? Must it, in the moment of realization that art is, be either particle *or* wave? Has modern art in some measure avoided that choosing? Has it managed, at times, to allow it to be both particle *and* wave, location *and* motion?

Classical physics—and, it seems to me, most of premodern art—focused on a grammar of knowing that *chooses*, a grammar of seeing/saying/judging that accepts, even declares, the adequacy of *one* aspect—as measure of reality, as measure of truth. And surely one of the principal dangers of the merely conventional in art resides precisely in its long association with that grammar of seeing and saying. In poetry, for instance, the music of conventional seeing and saying is always a potential pull of the poet toward a fixing of the physical world somewhere—pointing to it, locating it. As instrument of style, it resists the poet's attempts to hear other stresses, further accents; accents that might sound the word's participation in the very structure of reality; might reveal the word as, indeed, experience of that structure (itself a system of probabilities) even as it takes physical, locational form—in the mouth, on the page.

Has language, by its very nature, always been the means by which we can "experience" the inherently quantum nature of reality, always standing with one foot in the ocean of being, the other in the river of meaning? Have words, within the structure of language, been the means whereby reality's dual nature—matter and not-matter, conscious and unconscious, fixed and in motion—is always revealed?

Perhaps. But is not poetry necessary to the fulfillment of that potential? How else fully experience its transformational quality—being becoming becoming, becoming becoming being?—resisting the grammar of completion, struggling against the syntax of certainty. . . . Is it not possible to see this aspect of mind in the twentieth century expressing itself, revealing itself, in the poetry?

"Poetry," wrote Jacques Maritain, "is that intercommunication between the inner being of things and the inner being of the human self." This profound statement about the nature of poetry—about the very being of poetry—offers, I believe, a useful perspective from which to view the true "modernity," the radical "seeing," of, for instance, William Carlos Williams's poetry. In Williams, much of what the lines offer is not so much something perceived as it is actual perception occurring, the moment of "intercommunication" itself. The issue is not something seen, but seeing occurring, both perception and perceived revealed.

Consider, for example, this intriguing poem from *The Clouds*:

THE MIND HESITANT

Sometimes the river
becomes a river in the mind
or of the mind
or in and of the mind

Its banks snow
the tide falling a dark
rim lies between
the water and the shore

And the mind hesitant
regarding the stream
senses
a likeness which it

will find—a complex
image: something

of white brows
bound by a ribbon

of sooty thought
beyond, yes well beyond
the mobile features
of swiftly

flowing waters, before
the tide will
change
and rise again, maybe

All of this poem, to be sure, is in action—*is* action, rather than report. But most important, perhaps, is that the lines equally insist both across and down the page—horizontals and verticals—never quite choosing between the two, engaged in their enactment of the basic evocation of both being and seeing, their importance always exceeding their mere participation in statement, always striving to reach toward something more basic, more perceptually elemental, something beyond the grammar and syntax of the world of objects and classical physics.

Paradoxically, out of this striving emerges a world at once less objective and more physical.

Nowhere, I think, is this more apparent than in that seminal and truly original book *Spring and All*. The burden of this book, clearly, is to explore this vision—this new vision—through poems that express it and through attempts to comment on the matrix of thought/experience/perception that the poems arise out of. And which they embody.

"The only realism in art is of the imagination. It is only thus that the work escapes plagiarism after nature and becomes a creation.

"Invention of new forms to embody this reality of art, the one thing which art is, must occupy all serious minds concerned." This from *Spring and All*.

As is this (from poem XXIII):

> The veritable night
> of wires and stars
>
> the moon is in
> the oak tree's crotch
>
> and sleepers in
> the windows cough
>
> athwart the round
> and pointed leaves
>
> and insects sting
> while on the grass
>
> the whitish moonlight
> tearfully
>
> assumes the attitudes
> of afternoon—
>
> But it is real
> where peaches hang . . .

Even the syntax of this poetry is alive to the swift, electronic change and interchange, phenomena always immersed in flux and metamorphosis, always in the motion of occurrence. This quality of the poem participates in what constitutes, overall, "movements of the imagination revealed in words"; it is part and aspect of the total formal exploration of this new work, which results in, as Williams puts it, "new form dealt with as a reality in itself."

And of course this new form is a reality which sees itself differently. It is a form alive to the awareness of the both/and picture of reality that both science and philosophy have been led to, not the either/or perception that underlies the formal investigations and expressions of earlier periods (mind *or* body, objective *or* subjective, place *or* movement, particle *or* wave).

And it is a form that rejects perforce any naive view of the poem's relationship to an "external" reality.

In great works of the imagination *A CREATIVE FORCE IS SHOWN AT WORK MAKING OBJECTS WHICH ALONE COMPLETE SCIENCE AND ALLOW INTELLIGENCE TO SURVIVE.*

— Spring and All

But perhaps nowhere in poetry can the quality of this new awareness be seen more clearly than in the work of George Oppen. In a poem such as "If It All Went Up in Smoke," for example, we find a poetry that is striving to see at the very edge of perception, one that is striving to push language toward a grammar and syntax more sensitive to what quantum thinking demands of us.

IF IT ALL WENT UP IN SMOKE

that smoke
would remain

the forever
savage country poem's light borrowed

light of the landscape and one's footprints praise

from distance
in the close
crowd all

that is strange the source

the wells the poem begins

neither in word
nor meaning but the small
selves haunting

us in the stones and is less

always than that help me I am
of that people the grass

blades touch

and touch in their small

distances the poem
begins

Everywhere in this poem the syntax is immersed in metamorphosis, in transformation. It is a syntax completely open to contradiction. Backwards and forwards the syntax runs, both within the individual lines as well as between them. And we are touched by these complications, these further reaches into meaning. For we recognize—we feel—how they touch the unseen linkages, the lasting/vanishing connections among the world's small selves. Even more, we realize that these movements, these changes, are happening at some truly primary level of world's restless becoming, word's restless becoming—somewhere just below, or perhaps just prior to, the arrival of perceived phenomena. In other words, it's as if we actually see here being's great boil into awareness.

The roots of words
Dim in the subways

There is madness in the number
Of the living
"A state of matter"

There is nobody here but us chickens

Anti-ontology—

He wants to say
His life is real,
No one can say why

It is not easy to speak

A ferocious mumbling, in public
Of rootless speech
– no. 17, from "Of Being Numerous"

It is a haunting poetry that is thus produced, one in which our involvement in the awesomely swift rush of things—the rush together, the rush apart—is perceived at such a primary level of existence that we feel it as the very presence of our selves.

And there is, as the poem "Rationality" says, "no 'cure' / Of it." This is, simply, the condition of our lives. Here, the poems reveal, is the present experience of our selves, our own small selves:

> there is no "cure"
> Of it, a reversal
> Of some wrong decision—merely
> The length of time that has passed
> And the accumulation of knowledge.
>
> To say again: the massive heart
> Of the present, the presence
> Of the machine tools
>
> In the factories, and the young workman
> Elated among the men
> Is homesick
>
> In that instant
> Of the shock
> Of the press
>
> In which the manufactured part
>
> New in its oil
> On the steel bed is caught
> In the obstinate links
>
> Of cause, like the earth tilting
> To its famous Summers—that "part
>
> of consciousness" . . .

"The imagination," says Williams, "uses the phraseology of science. It attacks, stirs, animates, is radio-active in all that can be touched by action. Words occur in liberation by virtue of its processes."

Or as Oppen once wrote in a notebook, "Each WORD MUST BECOME SOLITARY." This is a challenging statement, one that keeps pulling one along toward further possibilities. But surely one strong implication of the statement is that the word must be allowed to be other than merely an element in the forward and defining march of grammar and syntax. In other words, in order that it not be only a part of an either/or declaration, the poet must be willing to experience it also as participant in a wave of probability and potential. At some level Oppen seems to have understood that unless each word is accorded this both/and existence, there will be much less possibility of a poem's actually perceiving—and revealing—our participation in potential's emergence into form, matter into world.

But of course "form is not a 'shape' but an 'image,'" as Charles Simic has said, "the way in which my inwardness seeks visibility." Likewise, the kind of "seeing" that I have been trying to describe, a seeing that actually participates somehow in the quantum level of reality as well as in, simultaneously, the phenomenal one—such seeing does not require the shape of one particular "style," one form of poetry. In other words, it is surely likely that poems may find other ways of experiencing—and expressing—this seeing than those found by, say, Williams or Oppen. Is it not possible that in a poetry radically different in "shape" from those models we may find another, a different, engagement of this aspect of mind in the late twentieth century?

What, for instance, of the poems in Robert Hass's book *Human Wishes*? Could it be that we find there, particularly in what appear to be "prose poems," something which though obviously different is much the same? In these poems I suspect what we find is not so much a saying that is open to contradiction as a seeing that is so: I mean a seeing on the page—a visual display, we might say, of its own ambivalence. For in these poems which display themselves on the page like prose, we soon become aware not only of a recognizable verse presence working steadily through the lines, but also of the emergence of lines in our consciousness as lines, those integral visual-aural units we think of when we think "line."

Consider these opening lines of the book's title poem:

This morning the sun rose over the garden wall and a rare blue sky leaped from east to west. Man is altogether desire, say the Upanishads. Worth anything, a blue sky, says Mr. Acker, the Shelford gardener. Not altogether. In the end. Last night on television the ethnologist and the cameraman watched with hushed wonder while the chimpanzee carefully stripped a willow branch and inserted it into the anthill. He desired red ants. When they crawled slowly up the branch, he ate them, pinched between long fingers as the zoom lens enlarged his face. Sometimes he stopped to examine one, as if he were a judge at an ant beauty contest or God puzzled suddenly by the idea of suffering. There was an empty place in the universe where that branch wasn't and the chimp filled it . . .

Again and again the line breaks stand forth not as silent expressions of a prose printing convention, but rather as part of the voice of the poem, moments that participate in the poem's continual alternation between horizontal and vertical; moments that struggle against habit's expectations.

What we feel here—what we sense here, we might say—is the poet's refusal (the poem's refusal) to choose between prose and verse, between statement and act. But it is a true refusal, so that what we find is not a prose poem, in the conventional sense of the term, nor "rhythmic prose"—for these are not, it seems to me, prose rhythms—but what is, on the page, in some sense both. We can, of course, stop and examine it as verse and discover genuine patterns of regularity—say in syllable count per line, or in stresses per line, or even, in some instances, moments of almost pure metricality.

All day you didn't cry or cry out and you felt like sleeping. The desire to sleep was light bulbs dimming as a powerful appliance kicks on. You recognized that.   (from "Tall Windows")

Or:

> . . . Vision of Jack kneeling under the fig tree, palms
> prayerfully touching, looking up awed and reverent into the branches
> where the fat green figs hung like so many scrotums among the leaves.
> Scrota? But they were less differentiated than that: breasts, bottoms.
> The sexual ambiguity of flowers and fruits in French botanical drawings.
> Oh yes, sweet hermaphrodite peaches and the glister of plums
>
> (from "Conversion")

But when we do so examine them, the page's visual insistence
on the syntax of verticality—its immersion in the forward
thrust of prose formally revealed on the page—this undeniable
feature of the poem's form is correspondingly devalued; just
as the opposite is true if we somehow remain unaware of or
inattentive to the presence of verse within the lines we see and
say there.

I wonder whether another way of thinking about what is
happening in this poetry might be in terms of the opportunity
it offers for new recognitions of the role of chance in art—
chance encountered, for instance, via printing conventions, or
through page-making conventions, as it enters the poet's consciousness and offers new possibilities to his (and our) seeing:

> The two couples having dinner on Saturday night—it is late fall—are in
> their late thirties and stylish, but not slavishly so. The main course is
> French, loin of pork, probably, with a North African accent, and very
> good. The dessert will be sweet and fresh, having to do with cream and
> berries (it is early fall), and it feels like a course, it is that substantial.
>
> (from "Quartet")

Maybe so. Maybe not. One can't know for sure.

What does seem clear, however—and what is surely most
important—is that in some fundamental way this quality
participates in the poems' complexity of tone, a tone that is
haunted by the awful ambiguity and ambivalence of our lives
("it is late fall . . . it is early fall"), the yearnings and inclarities
that saturate and surround them ("it feels like a course, it is
that substantial"). Or as we see it in the poem "January":

Rachel is looking for a house. A realtor had just shown her one. Looking at the new house, she loved the old one, especially the green of the garden, looking out on the garden. The old house has drawbacks, long rehearsed, and the new one, with its cedar shingles, exposed beams, view, doesn't feel right, it is so anonymous and perfect; it doesn't have the green secrecy of the garden or the apple tree to tie Lucia's swing to. Earlene is asking questions, trying to help. A few minutes later, when I pass through again, they are laughing. At the comedy in the business of trying to sort through mutually exclusive alternatives in which figures some tacit imagination of contentment, some invisible symbolizing need from which life wants to flower. "I hate that old house," Rachel is saying, laughing, tears in her eyes. But that is not mainly what I notice; I find myself looking at the women's skin, the coloring, and the first relaxation of the tautness of the sleeker skin of the young, the casual beauty and formality of that first softening.

Again and again these poems express their great longing for the world's body, its sensual, beautiful forms, the enclosing skin through which we touch it and touch it . . . And yet as they move inevitably through the rhetoric of their own perceptions they find themselves forced to let go and let go, to modify and abandon.

This is a quality, in other words, that participates in these poems' ability to resist making the limited—and limiting— choices (moral, perceptual, intellectual) that always offer themselves, in poems, in life—the horizontal integrity of the line here continuing to hold back, to resist, the plunge of language down the page of our mind: to decision, to statement, to judgment, to stillness; even as poetry enables words, on the horizon of their being, to continue to hold out against the powerful gravity of context as it tugs and tugs them steadily toward conclusion.

To this extent, and in this way, this quality participates in the means these particular poems seem to have found of experiencing the complex involvement in the life of the spirit that verse has been immersed in during this century, as poetry has attempted to discover, on the page, the living reality we and the planet are together.

Thus these poems too seem to incorporate that fundamental condition of our lives which we have been discussing; I mean that inevitable antagonism we exist as, always caught between contending forces, vertical and horizontal, statement and enactment, movement and location, meaning and value:

> the crux
> we stand erect
>
> and lie down
> as

Dreams, Myth, Poetry

What is perhaps most amazing about the mind in the act of dreaming is the fluent and instantaneous way it creates (or recreates)—seemingly with no need for revision—a world complete in itself: irreducible, untranslatable, alive with its own spiritual force. Full with its own spiritual force. As far as I can tell, we are getting no nearer to any real understanding of this awesome—and basic—fact of the mind, despite all the recent efforts directed toward "scientific" studies of sleep and dreaming. And the simple fact remains: the patterns of our dreams are often those of myth, wherever and whenever encountered.

A profound question for poets, one which tantalizes and beckons them on, is "How can one, when awake, gain access to that fluency, that power and fullness, that mode of perception/ creation in which there is no gap whatever, no time lag, however brief, between thought (or perception) and its content?" No doubt some people dream more interesting dreams than others. And of course the dreams of any person on a given night may be more interesting, or fuller, than on another night. But in general it is clear that if we could, waking, have full access to that fluency and simultaneity of the mind, our every moment of thinking would be literature, would be art—or at least what we in the absence of that capacity strive for in art.

We of course make such encounters, know such instances of oneness, in rare moments: in myth, in dreams, in art. It was some such perception as this that Picasso—and others—made early in this century when they saw, for the first time, "primitive" art. And present in this perception was, clearly, a recognition of the essential oneness of human experience, when encountered at moments of fullness—a oneness that reaches across millennia and cultures to touch, as if by magic, that mythic center of human being. Picasso, we know, saw it as, for the artist, power, the power to reach, instantaneously, to the unconscious spirit pool every man or woman shares, across gulfs of time and space, with every other—the incandescent experience, in an instant of time, of what is perduringly human.

And is not that instant, that moment of timeless humanity, also necessarily one of linkage? with the earth we live—and die—on; with the animals we share the mystery of life with, and whose experience of fear and pain and death is so close to our own that their familiar eyes haunt us as we sleep; with the trees and grass that catch—and change—our breath as we move among them, even in dream; linkage with the places we are, the physical and spiritual phenomena our lives describe.

✳

Freud observes that in the test of the reality of a perception, the important thing is not to find "in reality" something that the perception accurately corresponds to. For the point is not to copy something but to reinvent it, reinvent it so that what is perceived actually *feels* true, and so that one can therefore believe in continuance, which is to say, believe in the continued being of the world. And of ourselves.

In poetry, it seems to me, reinvention has inescapably as one of its ingredients feeling. How the phenomenal world feels to me, as it is made available through my senses, is what makes it (remembered/imagined) seem true, makes it feel actual, continuing; makes it exist, have irreducible being. Like the world itself, of course, but also like dreams.

*

But what incorporates that feeling, what embodies it? Is it not, as has often been said, at least in part the rhythm (together with attendant matters such as sound), in short the music of the poem—concerns we are "unconscious" of, because they are, along with image, language the unconscious knows, language it speaks through? Are not these the modes by which, when we are successful, we enter, for a time, the unconscious, with its fluent and synchronous knowledge of the appearing world?

> What, for instance,
> of the rhythms the brain
>
> responds to
> in dreaming? of rhythms as,
>
> even, aspects
> of the brain, its parts
>
> and their functions—the cerebrum,
> the cerebellum,
>
> the spinal cord and medulla
> oblongata, that soft
>
> spot we have
> inside us

for our own
bodies . . . And what

of the rhythms of
those bodies, awake

or sleeping, moving
on the earth?—rhythms

of remembered
patterns, within

and between us, words
reasserting themselves

each time
we speak, ourselves

uttering ourselves, in
and across

time; rhythms
of air and water

over our outspread
arms, their memories

deep inside
the cells of our bodies

❋

And then there is the "structure" that dreams share. Consider, for instance, how dreams tend to move, without narrative or explanatory connection, from one moment or event to the next, yet with the feeling that there *is* some kind of wholeness. Like the waking world, this one is real and unquestionable, multidimensional and irreducible. It exists, it has unity. It is both source and subject of thought. It is *presence* of feeling.

This has, in fact, also been the structure of much poetry,

especially in the twentieth century. For it has been recognized as a promising avenue into, however briefly, that reality the unconscious is.

Perhaps, then, dreaming is an instance of metaphor as narrative. It is also instance of that familiar pattern of the universal in the particular: going down, via the particular, to the everyone inside (a concept that is at the very heart of Freud's great insight that the individual psyche is the human psyche). For that too is mythos. And that is also ultimate metaphor, metaphor as moment of link—and perception.

*

The work of art, it may be, brings before the conscious mind a complete, or at least an adequate, presentation of unconscious knowing, so that we are able, for a time, to see that content, to feel it in its symbolic inexhaustibility, able to know its numinous authority.

Perhaps bringing successfully into a poem the feeling complex that is at once both its content and its source is a way of achieving, in art, a moment of integrity, integrity for what seems, ordinarily, dis- or unintegrated. But integration here does not mean resolution, or even understanding, in the sense that one has understood, and so exhausted, its meaning. Rather, it means that this rich and powerful dimension of one's life has been held for an instant—an eternal instant, perhaps—in relatively full view: the self glimpsing, in sun or shade, the self beyond.

Back to the Snowy Fields

Go back now thirty years later and you will still find it, lying silently in ditches beside the road, drifting noiselessly in with the snow at nightfall, standing dry and bristly in a field of weeds: *the spirit of the American prairie*. For that is what Robert Bly discovered for us in *Silence in the Snowy Fields*: the spirit of the American prairie landscape. Nowhere a trace, not one blurring linger, of language or perception from another culture or geography (all influences of Spanish, Chinese, Latin American—and other—poets not withstanding). Just the American land, breathing into and through Bly. And us. I would even go so far as to say, if pressed, that however much else Bly may have contributed to the ferment of American letters, this has been perhaps his most important contribution—aside from the rich offering of the poems themselves. Once we had experienced *Silence in the Snowy Fields*, the body of America was never again the same to us—never again "merely" there, never again *external* to our own locus of spirit, no longer obedient to even the most carefully translated commands from "English" poetry. Since *Silence,* a developing generation of new young poets has been able to take for granted the subtle and important knowledge of our geographical lives that these poems provide. It has come to be a given, something which, once gained, one can never go back from: like self-consciousness. It has become a fundamental fact of not just a *way* of knowing, but also a *what.*

But perhaps *consciousness* would be the more useful term, because it is *consciousness* that these poems are concerned with, consciousness of the world of solitude, of darkness, of isolation, of silence. That's what these poems are in touch with—the other world: sleep, the hidden, the unseen: what might be called *the rest of it.* That's what the silence is filled with, what it frees us for: the other half, the realm of dark knowledge, night. Here the fields and rural buildings open out into that large dimension of (our) being. "We are all asleep in the outward man," Bly quotes Boehme, as an epigraph for the book, then goes on to offer poems which, taken all together, call to us, *Wake up! Wake up!*—in and through the inward man. This is the persistent urge one feels in *Silence in the Snowy Fields*: the urge to spiritual perception. We sense the need to discover the other-dimensionality of being. "There is unknown dust that is near us," the poem "Surprised by Evening" begins, "Waves breaking on shores just over the hill, / Trees full of birds that we have never seen, / Nets drawn down with dark fish."

> The evening arrives; we look up and it is there,
> It has come through the nets of the stars,
> Through the tissues of the grass,
> Walking quietly over the asylums of the waters.

Everything, we sense, is fraught with incommensurably greater meaning. In a substantial number of these poems we have the overwhelming sense that somehow we have suddenly broken through a thin covering into a purely subjective landscape. And yet *it* is the one that seems more real; indeed, in those moments we believe that it is *the* real:

Now we wake, and rise from bed, and eat breakfast—
Shouts rise from the harbor of the blood,
Mist, and masts rising, the knock of wooden tackle in the
    sunlight.

Now we sing, and do tiny dances on the kitchen floor.
Our whole body is like a harbor at dawn
We know that our master has left us for the day.
                                    – "Waking from Sleep"

It is a pleasure, also, to be driving
Toward Chicago, near dark,
And see the lights in the barns.
The bare trees more dignified than ever,
Like a fierce man on his deathbed,
And the ditches along the road half full of private snow.
                                – "Three Kinds of Pleasures"

And in a poem such as "Return to Solitude" there is the implication that entire histories go on in a kind of subjective isolation, a place of solitude:

What shall we find when we return?
Friends changed, houses moved,
Trees perhaps, with new leaves.

There is an urgency about the moments and events in these
poems. Everything is darkly radiant with something which, Bly
manages to suggest, we urgently need to know.

The dusk has come, a glow in the west, as if seen through
the isinglass on old coal stoves, and the cows stand around
the barn door; now the farmer looks up at the paling sky
reminding him of death, and in the fields the bones of
the corn rustle faintly in the last wind, and the half moon
stands in the south.
    Now the lights from barn windows can be seen through
bare trees.
                                            – "Fall"

And at such times as these we don't know whether we fall, or rise, into greater awareness.

But of course the physical details, in Bly, are the essential ingredients, for they are the windows we see through, they are the doors we fall through, the vessels we find ourselves in.

TAKING THE HANDS

Taking the hands of someone you love,
You see they are delicate cages . . .
Tiny birds are singing
In the secluded prairies
And in the deep valleys of the hand.

The poems continually plunge inside: ourselves, the landscape, the face of the American prairie. The spiritual content, we feel, does not exist as some detached or detachable "significance"; it is the content of *this* body (or bodies): *these* places, *these* moments, *these* people. And if one should have a sudden epiphany, a lunge to an unconscious knowing of the gestalt of wholeness in some moment, it will likely be while driving toward the Lac Qui Parle River, through small towns with porches built right on the ground. Or while walking in a corn field. Or among odorous weeds. Authentic language, Bly says elsewhere, arises out of a depth, "coming up from . . . every source." And what Bly offers, in the images and language of these poems, is not an excess of originality, but an ecstasy of appropriateness and recognition.

A successful poem, it seems to me, can profitably be talked of as if it were a living thing, through and in whose body we find beauty, density, grace, *further* life. All bodies are different of course, as are all persons, all poems, all experiences. But even the most limited glimpse of a person's physical presence, the merest hint, can bring the whole of it rushing into our consciousness: the line of a neck, the sound of a familiar footstep, the lovely curve where hip rounds into flank—suddenly we know the whole of it: person, poem, place. In *Silence in the*

Snowy Fields the *whole* Bly is reaching for is that insistent sense of spiritual reality which the *family* of poems must identify. And we know what the family, individual in their bodies, will look like:

> The light was dawn. Like a man who has come home
> After seeing many dark rivers, and will soon go again,
> The dawn stood there with a quiet gaze;
> Our eyes met through the top leaves of the young ash.

> Dawn has come. The clouds floating in the east have turned white.
> The fence posts have stopped being a part of the darkness.
> The depth has disappeared from the puddles on the ground.
> I look up angrily at the light.
>   – "Getting Up Early"

Poem after poem in this remarkable book successfully enlarges a bare-bones narrative, exemplumlike in its simplicity, with an incomparably greater sense of existence, a complex presence of life. We come to be aware, as Bly is aware, of the abiding presence of a hidden order, the sacred masked by the ordinary. Poems arrive to suddenly opened vistas:

> We know the road; as the moonlight
> Lifts everything, so in a night like this
> The road goes on ahead, it is all clear.
>   – "After Working"

or to vague, indefinable threats:

> The barn is full of corn, and moving toward us now,
> Like a hulk blown toward us in a storm at sea;
> All the sailors on deck have been blind for many years.
>   – "Snowfall in the Afternoon"

For there *is* threat in *Silence.* Water:land, dark:daylight, waking:sleeping—these are the antinomies of our life the poems embody. And within the antinomies lies, often, a susceptibility to the forlornness in *Silence*:

> Something homeless is looking on the long roads—
> A dog lost since midnight, a small duck
> Among the odorous reeds,
> Or a tiny box-elder bug searching for the window pane.
> Even the young sunlight is lost on the window pane,
> Moving at night like a diver among the bare branches
>   silently lying on the floor.

Indeed there are times when it is impossible to tell whether the waking is a source more of gain or of loss. Even the beautiful and brilliant (and oft-quoted) "But, at last, the quiet waters of the night will rise, / And our skin shall see far off, as it does under water"—even this is, finally, ambiguous (I think richly so) in its emotional implication. There is a sense of *duende* about the darkness, "like a paling sky reminding [us] of death." So much happens in these poems at the very moment of shift— from day to night, from sleeping to waking, etc. Events suddenly open up like doors, and a world walks strangely and disturbingly in.

AFTERNOON SLEEP

I

I was descending from the mountains of sleep.
Asleep I had gazed east over a sunny field,
And sat on the running board of an old Model A.
I awoke happy, for I had dreamt of my wife,
And the loneliness hiding in grass and weeds
That lies near a man over thirty, and suddenly enters.

II

When Joe Sjolie grew tired, he sold his farm,
Even his bachelor rocker, and did not come back.
He left his dog behind in the cob shed.
The dog refused to take food from strangers.

III

I drove out to that farm when I awoke;
Alone on a hill, sheltered by trees.
The matted grass lay around the house.
When I climbed the porch, the door was open.
Inside were old abandoned books,
And instructions to Norwegian immigrants.

The movement back and forth between dreaming and waking, between unconscious and conscious is a fundamental one in these poems, as in "Remembering in Oslo the Old Picture of the Magna Carta":

The girl in a house dress, pushing open the window,
Is also the fat king sitting under the oak tree,
And garbage men, thumping their cans, are
Crows still cawing.
And the nobles are offering the sheet to the king.
One thing is also another thing, and the doomed galleons,
Hung with trinkets, hove by the coast, and in the blossoms
Of trees are still sailing on their long voyage from Spain;
I too am still shocking grain, as I did as a boy, dog tired,
And my great-grandfather steps on his ship.

Here is a move not only to unconscious knowing, but almost to a kind of *racial* knowledge, sweeping away differences of both time and space in the identification offered in the last two lines. And in a poem such as "Getting Up Early," we experience a form of double existence in ourselves. The poem has a sort of commutative effect, causing us suddenly to experience the potent flow of spiritual energy back and forth between the two poles, conscious and unconscious. Or the movement can lead to the momentary experience of pure timelessness, the extension of a perception into endless duration, as in "A Late Spring Day in My Life":

A silence hovers over the earth:
The grass lifts lightly in the heat

> Like the ancient wing of a bird.
> A horse gazes steadily at me.

Needless to say, the duration is achieved through the induction, via the images, of a flow at once into and outside of the speaker, as well as backward and forward in time, so that in the experience itself, inside and outside become one, as do past and present. Indeed, it might be worthwhile to note that a sort of reverie, a dreaming recovery, is frequently an effective instrument in these poems for evoking the unconscious.

> We want to go back, to return to the sea,
> The sea of solitary corridors,
> And halls of wild nights,
> Explosions of grief,
> Diving into the sea of death,
> Like the stars of the wheeling Bear.
>
> > – "Return to Solitude"

Memory (Mnemosyne), it should be remembered, was long ago identified as the mother of poetry. And rightly so. Surely a primary force in the impulse to poetry is the need to rescue the life of the individual spirit from the constant fall into unawareness, to recover, in M. L. Rosenthal's words, "past states of existence, isolated and framed and glowing with their own life as well as with the emotion that has recalled them—something in the present moment that is shared with the past state." Memory, reverie, the unconscious—they share, in some close, symbiotic way, a common, if at times dark, area of the human mind. Memory is perhaps like a heretofore missing conductor, now suddenly completing the circuit that makes possible the flow further into, and out of, ourselves—and our world. It provides in some way, I would guess, the emotional force field that makes possible a sense of temporal simultaneity and spatial diffusion. If poetry depends absolutely on its idiosyncratic truthfulness to the poet's own sense of reality, it depends equally on a powerful stroke of memory, memory of *the living quality* of an experience that in part was not a conscious experience. For Bly, in *Silence in the Snowy Fields*, this is memory of experience irradiated by meaning and significance—always in danger of being lost. And the poems continually put us in contact with an urgent sense of the numinous, out of which we wake (or fade) into *mere* existence. The second (or middle) section of *Silence* is entitled "Awakening," but the poems there lead one to an awakening that is more an awakening into, than out of, sleep. Here—in dreams, in reveries, in dark descents, in flights into the unconscious—we wake, paradoxically, into the other dimension of ourselves.

And always we are aware of our bodies—stiff-fingered and clumsy with cold, or alive like a harbor at dawn, or alert to the sound of corn stalks in the wind, to the dark pull of a spot of earth we could feel safe in, to the odor of leaves on the wet earth, to the feel of moonlight on our branches. And then we are, at last, fully inside the land of ourselves. "If I reached my hands down, near the earth," we say,

> I could take handfuls of darkness!
> A darkness was always there, which we never noted.

✳

So after *Silence in the Snowy Fields* we were never quite the same again. The darkness in us was never the same again. Nor the snow that covers the bare fields waiting always behind our eyes. Nor the barns we hold ourselves to the remembered earth by. Nor the houses we are adrift in—in Minnesota, Ohio, Michigan, Illinois, and elsewhere all over the great body of the land our breath freezes, and warms, in. Sometimes, now, a cowbell sounds from so deep within us, or the eyes of a horse gaze so clearly into our consciousness, that we wake suddenly into a present which *Silence in the Snowy Fields* seems always to have been a bright—and dark—part of.

The Art of Poetry and the
Temper of the Times

*The pestered and bedeviled spirit of man, bedeviled by the
deadly, lying repetitiousness of doctrinaire formula worship
which is the standard work of the day.*
— William Carlos Williams

*When truth and virtue are threatened, I must surrender even my
favorite jewels.*
— Lu Chi

In 1957, James Wright, of Martins Ferry, Ohio, published his first book of poems, entitled *The Green Wall*, which
was chosen by W. H. Auden for the Yale Younger Poets award
for that year. It was a book characterized by heavily "traditional" forms (including not only rhyme and meter, but also
its diction) and by those staple ingredients of new criticism—
inspired poetry, wit and irony. Critics such as Auden and
Thom Gunn heaped praise on Wright for his technique. Two
years later, Wright published his second book of poems, *St.
Judas*, which consisted of poetry in much the same vein. Some
even hailed him as "the new Keats."

But there were dissenting voices. James Dickey, for example,
reviewing for the *Sewanee Review*, tapped him for membership
in the "Poetic School of Charm." Richard Foster, in a review of
New Poets of England and America, singled out Wright's work as
a particularly good example of the use of technique in such a
way as to cloud all possibility of honesty and meaning.

Four years later, *The Branch Will not Break* was published, exhibiting and expressing the James Wright we came to admire and love over the next twenty years. And this was a new Wright, one who had moved from the forms and language of the English tradition to something at once more native and more daring.

But Wright did not come to this, to him, new approach without struggle and soul searching, without *personal* change. He had to learn to see himself differently, both as a man and as a poet: to see himself as a *perceiver* rather than an *imposer* of order and meaning; had to move from a poetry of fixity to a poetry of possibility. And he learned, as Kevin Stein puts it, to trust the music of natural speech. Thus it should not surprise us that he began to write, for the most part, an unrhymed and meterless verse. "Meter," John Crowe Ransom reminds us, "is not an original property of things. It is artificial and conveys the sense of human control." And James Wright had come to see himself as a democratically equal participant in Nature, not one either outside it or above it.

So James Wright joined a large number of his generation in their reassessment and reevaluation of themselves and their art. He also moved, in so doing, into what had been in fact a central movement in poetry in America for several decades. Years later Galway Kinnell would say, looking back on his own early poems: "It might have turned out better for me if, during that period of my life, I had written less and given myself more to silence and waiting. At least those arduous searches for the right iambic beat and rhyme word seem now like time that could have been better spent." As Lorca says, "The *duende* rejects all the sweet geometries one has learned, it breaks with all styles." Or to come back to native soil: Whitman writes, in the original preface to *Leaves of Grass*, "I will not have in my writing any elegance or effort or originality to hang in the way, not the richest curtains."

What these poets—what American poetry—had come to, or

come back to, was poetry of open, rather than closed, form. A poetry formally open to its possibilities, its discoveries; a poetry whose form (and that emphatically includes language) is *complicit* in its meaning. It is a poetry that knows the difference between meter and rhythm, knows that there are incomparably more rhythms than there are meters. Knows that a true native poetry, an American poetry, must have a sense of the rhythms we live by,

> rhythms that hold us
> to the earth.

And clearly this has marked the direction of American poetry during the last twenty-five years and more. It has given us the large and significant body of work of such poets as—in addition to Wright—A. R. Ammons, John Ashbery, Robert Bly, Robert Creeley, Louise Gluck, Michael Harper, Richard Hugo, Galway Kinnell, Denise Levertov, Philip Levine, William Matthews, W. S. Merwin, Mary Oliver, Adrienne Rich, Charles Simic, Louis Simpson, William Stafford, Gerald Stern, C. K. Williams, Charles Wright, to name only a double handful. It has given us a language rich and full in its contact with our own deepest lives, with our own names and places. Our own landscape. Listen to this poem by Robert Bly:

DRIVING TOWARD THE LAC QUI PARLE RIVER

I

I am driving; it is dusk; Minnesota.
The stubble field catches the last growth of sun.
The soybeans are breathing on all sides.
Old men are sitting before their houses on carseats
In the small towns. I am happy,
The moon rising above the turkey sheds.

II

The small world of the car
Plunges through the deep fields of the night,

On the road from Willmar to Milan.
This solitude covered with iron
Moves through the fields of night
Penetrated by the noise of crickets.

III

Nearly to Milan, suddenly a small bridge,
And water kneeling in the moonlight.
In small towns the houses are built right on the ground;
The lamplight falls on all fours in the grass.
When I reach the river, the full moon covers it;
A few people are talking low in a boat.

And this one by James Wright:

BEAUTIFUL OHIO

Those old winnebago men
Knew what they were singing.
All summer long and all alone,
I had found a way
To sit on a railroad tie
Above the sewer main.
It spilled a shining waterfall out of a pipe
Someone had gouged through the slanted earth.
Sixteen thousand and five hundred more or less people
In Martins Ferry, my home, my native country,
Quickened the river
With the speed of their lives
In the instant of that waterfall.
I know what we call it
Most of the time.
But I have my own song for it,
And sometimes, even today,
I call it beauty.

This is a poetry that *sounds* like us. And it has produced
poems that are the sentences which, living, we make, sounds

so personal to us they seem to come from everywhere inside our body. As Frost reminds us: "Remember that the sentence sound often says more than the words."

What this poetry reflects is an attitude, an uncompromising seriousness, about the difficult and noble art of imaginative writing. A seriousness that leads not to arrogance and a feeling of superiority but to openness: openness to the imagination; openness to freshness, to originality; openness to the spirit voicing itself bodily forth on the pages we become. I'm talking about poetry not as mere *expression* but as adventure of the spirit. I'm speaking about poetry as *enactment* of that adventure, that quest; about writing that is discovering, rather than imposing, meaning—pointing to and discovering the unknown, existent and real and inexhaustible, in both itself and ourselves. This is poetry that yields a language alive to all its meaning, purged of bluster and pretense and the egocentricity of the will: writing that is attentive to the music of the psyche, in and out of time.

*

A principal danger to poets and poetry these days, it seems to me, is the tendency to try to nail everything down, to remove all ambiguity, to get the final answer. I don't know where this tendency comes from. Perhaps it has always been there. Perhaps it is truly an expression of what we refer to when we say "human nature." But it may well be, too, that it is an expression of our age's increasing longing for the absolute, for the definitive, even as certainty after certainty is being swept away— *especially* as certainty after certainty is being swept away.

Consider: The Big Bang theory of the "creation" of the universe has recently come to be more and more a source of discomfort for some astronomers and astrophysicists because of the complications certain new discoveries and observations in distant galaxies have given rise to. As a result, some of those astronomers and astrophysicists are even beginning to suggest that the theory is "false," even as others (the majority still) declare that it is true—at least until something better comes along, something that, whatever else it might do, will equally well account for three fundamental facts: the apparent evenness of cosmic background radiation throughout the universe; the fact that the universe is expanding; and the fact that hydrogen and helium—Big Bang by-products both—make up almost all the matter in the universe.

Nothing new in this "scientific" approach to reconciling fact and theory, of course. I cite it as simply another instance of how *either/or* continue to be the horns of our theorizing about ourselves, and the universe we live in. Often the oversimplifying horns. Polarization in discussion often takes place quite literally even before discussion begins, so that what we intended to be—and often still call—"discussion" becomes, simply, argument. In discussions of poetry nowadays, increasingly one notices a stiffening of resistance to suggestions that poets, and indeed cultures, need continually to examine, to question, their assumptions. And the observation that an "existing rhetoric" is one which *by its very nature* tends to mask its own assumptions— such a suggestion nowadays frequently provokes a seemingly involuntary resistance, if not a downright hostility.

Yet it seems to me that what is crucial to poetry—and to the poet—is the willingness to question, and to challenge, one's own assumptions; that is, the willingness to question the actual "rhetoric" of one's beliefs and preconceptions.

The majority of poets in our time seem to have felt both that need and that willingness. They seem to have felt, with Barthelme, the need to "silence" that existing rhetoric—not in order to better "control" one's poem, which a poet friend of mine recently automatically "assumed" would be the point of the silencing, but rather in order that the poem (that purest of relationships with the word itself) might be set free from the mere either/or-ness of argument, of debate, of assertion, of partiality; that it might be set free, in short, to experience the enormous complexity—the mystery—of a language in which, for example, the Big Bang theory might somehow be both true and not true; a language in which mind-and-matter's emergence into song is an experience infinitely beyond the capacity of "fashion" in poetry ever to compass.

✳

For the past several years now there has been a growing tone of anger and hostility and intolerance in many of the pronouncements about the state of poetry today. In magazines and books throughout the land have appeared essays bemoaning the slackness of American poetry over the past two decades, pointing an accusing finger at the (putative) absence of "traditional" forms and meters, as if this were prima facie evidence of demonic possession. Or the decline of Western culture. Or the death of poetry.

One hears that same tone, that same intellectual (and aesthetic) intolerance elsewhere, too. I think I even heard something similar recently when my wife and I visited the Museum of Modern Art in New York City. At one point we found ourselves in the Abstract Expressionists Room, almost alone with the works of some of the major figures in this important movement in American painting: Rothko, Pollack, Motherwell. Only two other couples were in the room, one older, one younger.

"I blame their teachers," the older woman was saying, "for telling them—for making them believe—that this is art, that there is any beauty in this."

"They should all be ashamed," the older man added.

And then, lest they be thought Philistines, I suppose, the woman said: "We've been going to modern art museums for over twenty years."

Similarly, one hears from certain quarters nowadays the charge that young poets are not being taught to work in "traditional" forms. But of course the truly serious question to ask here would be, "the forms of *what* tradition?" What about the predominant tradition of American poetry of this century, into which has fed the entire rich past of Classical, English, and Continental—as well as Chinese and Native American—art and thought? And also into which has fed this century's knowledge and speculation about the "reality" of our world, and our experience of it. Surely *that* is the tradition we should be aware of, must be aware of; one we must learn to understand and work in—and to value adequately. Its goal is not art as entertainment or embellishment or decoration, or even as, primarily, cultural expression, least of all as expression of one exclusive culture. It is perhaps closer to what Joseph Brodsky was attempting to define when he said:

> Poetry . . . is neither an art nor a branch of art but something a lot more crucial. If what distinguishes us from other species is speech, then poetry, which is the supreme version of language, is nothing less than our anthropological goal. Conversely, whoever regards poetry as . . . a form of entertainment, commits an anthropological crime, first of all against himself.

Only the most undiscriminating and insensitive could seriously imagine that such an attitude toward poetry could be served by a reduction of the problem to some simplified either/or concerning rhythm, or verse forms, or any other of the formal attributes poems live in.

This new reactionary zeal worries me. I know it is the zeitgeist, the temper of the times; but that is no consolation. Intolerance and mean-spiritedness are as dangerous in literature as in politics and religion. I am worried that these responses seem to be all a part of the same "cultural" movement, worried that they are instances of a new outbreak of an old "know-nothingism" which is now attacking us like a polio of the spirit—not just a nostalgia for the now-simplified problems and solutions of the past (which were anything but simple when the past was the present), but an actual refusal to recognize the complex and vital problems of the present; a reactionary and revisionist response that is simply inadequate to our truest lives.

What, one feels moved to ask, has happened to an awareness of the excited and exciting, yet anguished and anguishing, search for "truth," about ourselves and about our world, which was the drive to modernism? As Laszlo Géfin points out (*Ideogram: The History of a Method*), "The modernist revolution was closely related to the new vision of the universe provided by Einstein, Planck, and the 'new atomists' (Rutherford, Bohr, Schrodinger, Heisenberg) as well as the findings of archaeologists and anthropologists." Relativity. Uncertainty. Phenomenology. So far as I am aware, that is still the world we know, the world that responsible, serious, informed thought engages and expresses. To deny its reality, indeed its primacy, does not change those profound facts. And the longing for a simpler world and time, and for an artistic expression of such a simpler world, does not constitute a responsible alternative. As Owen Barfield once said, drowning should not be considered a form of swimming just because it is something you do in the water.

Form in a poem has not only ontological but also epistemological value. This, it seems to me, is crucial in poetry. It is what distinguishes poetry that matters from the always large mass of work that doesn't, true art from mere writing. As far as I'm concerned, this is what one *must* reach for in his/her art, the only kind of search that matters and the only kind of artistic embodiment that will be truly self-authenticating and sustaining. It's the only way form can rise to spiritual presence, the only way it can participate in *being*: enclose it, inform it, embody it. It's what Peter Stitt is trying to point to in Charles Wright's work when he writes (in the *Georgia Review*), "Somehow the form of the search is its own answer." Wright himself says,

> It's linkage I'm talking about,
> > and harmonies and structures
> And all the various things that lock our wrists to the past.
> Something infinite behind everything appears,
> > and then disappears.
> It's all a matter of how
> > you narrow the surfaces.
> It's all a matter of how you fit in the sky.

It's all a matter of trying to see, momentarily, wholeness. But this is not a "knowledge" that precedes or lies outside the poem. This is the knowledge that the poem *is*, the knowledge that the work of art is. And that knowledge exists only there, though it can *be* there only because there is connection between self and not-self, between the subjective and the objective world. But for the form to *be*, for it to participate in fullness, it must have this existential function, must be moment of epistemology.

Technique, Pound said, is the test of a poet's sincerity. An increasing percentage of the poems one sees these days lack, in this sense, sincerity. The technique betrays them: their devotion to "what adds up"—rationally. All the great insights and discoveries about the role and the fundamental importance of the unconscious and the irrational, which much of the art of this century has explored—all this is increasingly ignored, in danger of being abandoned or lost sight of because of lack of awareness and understanding. Some of our newer critics have in fact totally reversed the meaning of the term "sincerity" in their criticism. It has become, for them, a term of opprobrium. Their call is for more "objective," i.e., easier—and less valid— tests of authenticity. *Go back,* they cry, *to the good old tests of yesteryear. Where are his credentials? What are his credentials? Can he write a sonnet? How about some difficult-to-write language, language that dazzles, that shows "skill." More meter!* they cry. *Sincerity? Merely an excuse for sloppiness.*

But of course the longing there expressed is not just to go back to a time before the uncertainties and complexities of modernism: It is to go back even further, back beyond (that is, before) Romanticism. For it is a longing based on the triumph of materialism. Writing about form, Emerson said that it is a manner of thought "so passionate and alive that it creates an architecture of its own, and adorns nature with a new thing."

In our art we are, I believe, interested in the way the world works, and in the way the mind works. We want, even, to discover unity, to find, in other words, that "mind" and "world" are—subatomically, so to speak—identical. What the poem always wants to find out, in the serious gesture of art, is that they are identical. Here I think we are talking about physics as much as about poetic form.

But as Emerson pointed out, speaking of the materialistic thinkers of his day, "The intellectual men do not believe in any essential dependence of the material world on thought and volition." And so he makes a clear connection between materialism and the absence of "free" thinking, which is to say, the absence of *formal* thinking, thinking that is free from the imprisoning effect—the prior restraint—of nostalgia, of sentimentality, of convention masquerading as eternal and abiding truth.

The *duende*, Lorca reminds us, is at the heart of the most powerful poetry. The magical quality of a poem, he says, consists in its being always possessed by the *duende*, so that "whoever beholds it is baptized with dark water." Form without existential function, form not involved in and instinct with mortality, is itself an excuse: an excuse *from* final seriousness. And so art becomes amusement, decoration, cultural embellishment. This may be the way to promotion and pay (to borrow from Kipling), but it's not the way to important, or even serious, poetry.

So that's the climate we're moving into these days—in already, it seems to me. And it's a disheartening one. It has always been hard to be a good poet, I think. Maybe in this climate it will be even harder—harder to be a strong one, trying to write poems that matter, poems that attempt to share and embody the beautiful and terrifying mystery our lives are. Popularity has never been a test of anything other than popularity. Poetry sustains only to the extent that it pursues a more demanding, a more ambitious goal. *Art* is what we must seek, for it is measure—and instrument—of our life in the world, our connection with the universe we live in forever.